FREAK LIKE ME

Disclaimer

This book is intended for mature audiences only. It contains graphic scenes that are not appropriate for minors, the fainthearted, or the easily grossed out. They are human marvels, daredevils, people who have spent years disciplining their body or learning ancient knowledge, and freaks willing to do those things your mother always said you shouldn't.

FREAK LIKE ME

INSIDE THE JIM ROSE CIRCUS SIDESHOW

JIM ROSE

with MELISSA ROSSI

with an introduction
by KATHERINE DUNN

INDIGO

First Published in Great Britain 1996
by Indigo

Indigo is an imprint of the Cassell Group
Wellington House, 125 Strand, London WC2R 0BB

A catalogue record for this book is available from the British Library

ISBN 0 575 40033 1

Designed and typeset
by Fishtail Design

Printed by The Guernsey Press Co Ltd
Guernsey, Channel Isles

99 98 97 96 10 9 8 7 6 5 4 3 2 1

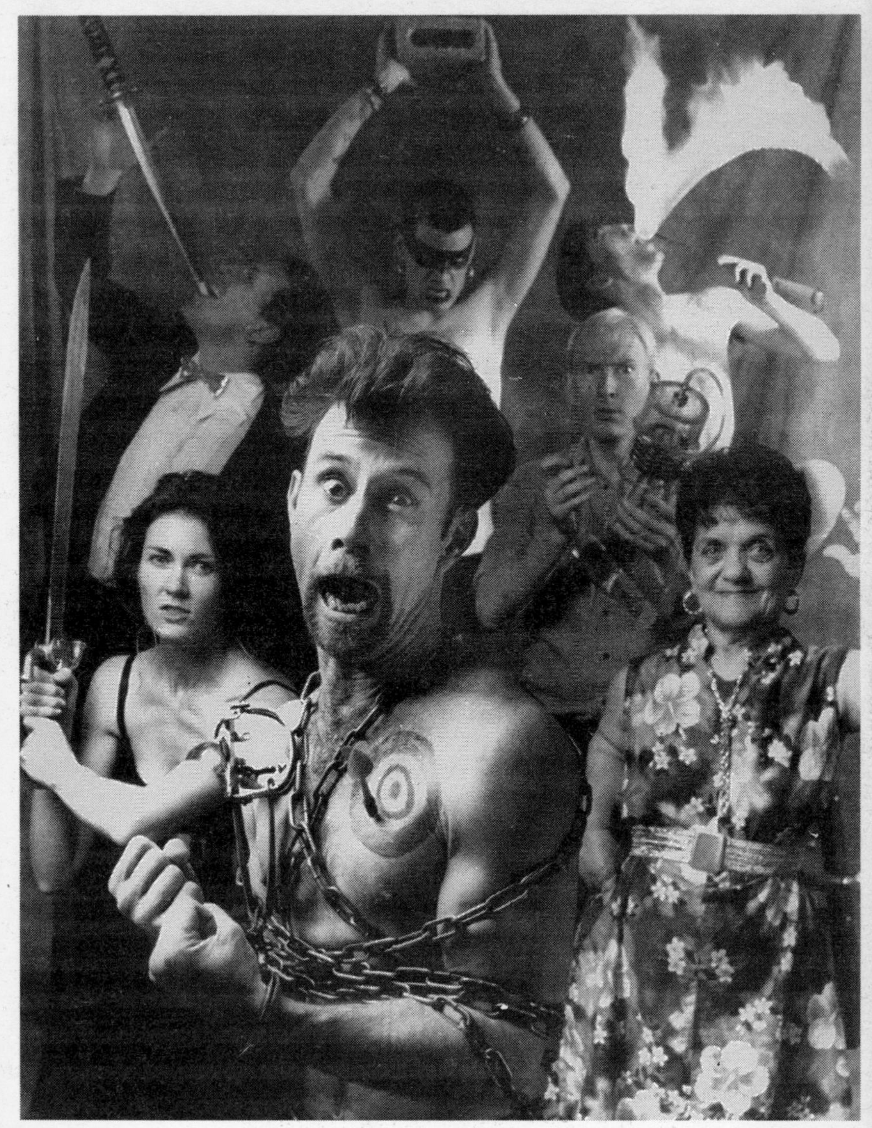

Jim Rose Circus Sideshow 1992.
Photo by Mark Van-S, Seattle WA.

This book is dedicated to Bebe Rose – Bebe the Circus Queen Rose – my wife. Without her magic, nothing would exist.

Special Thanks to:

Ruby Rose, Pat Peach, Russ Fega, Bill Judson, Chuck Dixon, Keith Christensen, [symbol], Sandra Elliot, Keith Naisbitt, Perry Ferrel, Vince O'Brien, Alison Braun, Tim Tom, Danny Clinch, Daryl Beckman, Sheila Lyon, Micky Hades, Mark Finkbine, Frank Weipert, Susie Bridges, Tom Phalen, Victoria Zatuvern, Stephany at Crocodile Café, Graham at Moe's, Kevin Statham, Mark Bukowski, Ted Mico, Julie Anderson, Darlene Dixon, Patrick Panzarella, Don Mueller, Henry Root, Lee Smith, Peter Barsotti, Melissa Dragich, Michael Chugg, Gary Cormier, Janeane Ardolino, Gary Knight and Melissa Rossi.

A Note to the Reader

As you read the following pages, you may have occasion to wonder, 'Are these stories for real?' Actually, yes they are. In a few instances, however, there have been slight alterations. Details have been omitted, time has been shrunk and a few events have been chronologically rearranged, a name or two has been changed to protect the guilty, other names have alas been forgotten.

And the stunts that you are going to read about are real, and can cause grave bodily harm if tried. Please do not try them at home. Anyone learning these tricks must practise under the supervision of a master, and even then it's a risky business.

CONTENTS

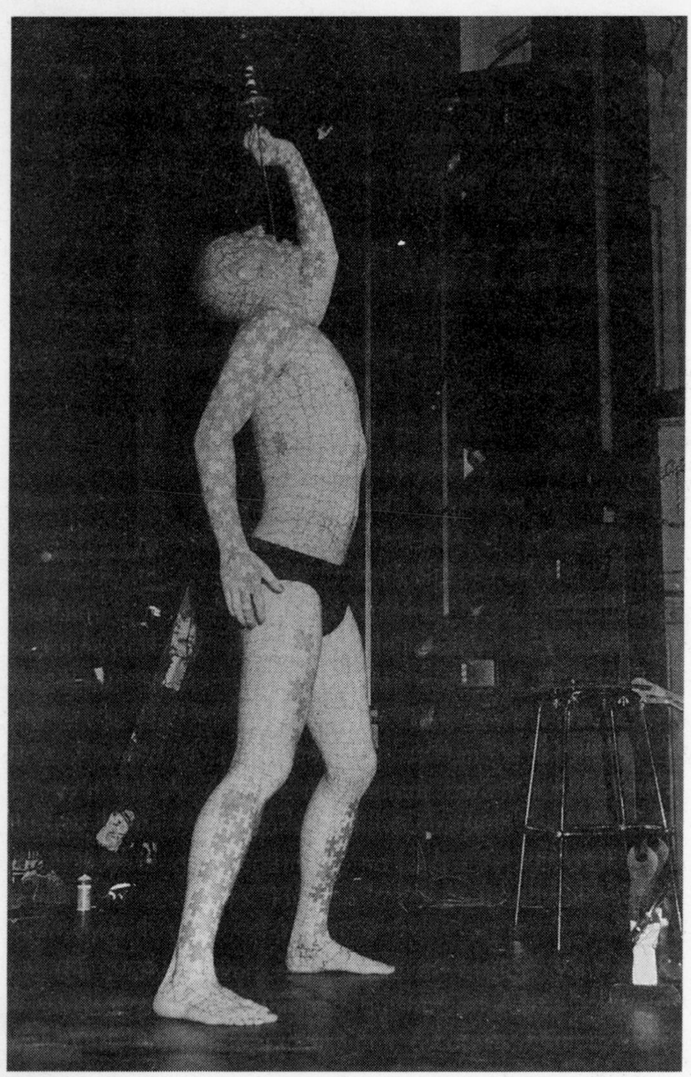

Enigma swallowing a sword.
Photo by David Harradine

INTRODUCTION

by Katherine Dunn

For practical purposes the word 'humane' means death. It is the polite word linked with gassing stray dogs rather than clubbing or starving them, and with sentencing evildoers to the electric chair rather than burning them at the stake. Wherever that word appears, something dies. So it was with the old-time travelling sideshows in America. The tent spectacles that gave our great-aunties palpitations died off in the 1950s. They were victims of a wave of prim disgust masquerading as humane sensitivity.

With the shows gone their human attractions sank into oblivion. 'Freaks of nature' – the Siamese twins, bearded ladies, three-legged Scotsmen – no longer exploited and no longer paid, retired to Floridian trailer parks or institutional mouldering.

The 'Marvels' were regular humans exploring the limits of physical possibility through ancient art forms – sword swallowers, fire eaters, pincushions, escapists, contortionists and geeks.

The Marvels' stock in trade was defying pain, pitting skill

against blatant danger to trigger a sympathetic fleshly anxiety in the audience. The term 'geek' originally referred to the guy who shocked the paying customers by biting the heads off live chickens. When early animal-rights activists protested at the torture of chickens, 'geek' acts expanded to include less engaging critters, from bugs to rats, and gradually came to mean all acts (anything involving snakes, for instance) whose primary appeal was not just fear but stomach-churning revulsion – the total gross-out.

A few of the more sanitary Marvels went to work in the centre rings of the few remaining circuses. The rest submerged in obscurity disguised as window washers, haberdashers or insurance adjusters.

After a while even the sideshow language was distorted and co-opted. The flower and pot children of the 60s and 70s called themselves freaks, and went on claiming the label long after they'd reverted to paying taxes and running for the school board. By the 1980s a geek was someone you wouldn't date, a guy with a personality problem.

Real freaks of nature still occur, though they are usually sequestered from public view. The Marvels are also far from extinct. In 1989 RE/SEARCH publications of San Francisco brought out *Modern Primitives*, a remarkable book exploring a thriving American subculture dedicated to tattoos, piercing and scarification. Inspired by the scholarship of the American Fakir Musafar, *Modern Primitives* had an enormous impact on the underground and avant-garde art world. Ancient forms of body modification mingling a spectrum of spiritual quests and political statements emerged in the rock-music scene and spread rapidly.

One side effect of the *Modern Primitives* consciousness

was recognition of the origins of the sideshow Marvels in Eastern religious rituals. The unlikely propagator of this particular linkage of centuries and cultures was a raunchy, edge-dancing, technohip showman named Jim Rose.

I live in Portland, Oregon, a few hundred miles from Jim's Seattle launch zone. The first time I ever heard his name was by telephone in the fall of 1991, a few weeks before I was scheduled to do a churchy literary reading at the University of Washington. The woman on the phone from the university obviously figured me for a sensitive artiste and was terrified of offending me. There was this man named Jim Rose, she stuttered, who had a weird kind of circus freak show, and he had offered to do a free performance at my reading because he liked my circus novel, *Geek Love*. Swell, I said, that ought to liven things up considerably. Her estimate of my artistic credentials had obviously been revised downwards by the time she hung up.

A week or so later, hearing that the Jim Rose Circus Sideshow was doing the opening of a Zebra Club clothing store in Portland, I decided to sneak an advance peek. The kerb out front was lined with big shiny Harleys. The groans and shrieks from inside meant the show was already on. There was a roar as I approached, and a burly biker staggered out the door, eyes bulging, sweat popping above his beard. He fell against the wall, gasping. 'Are you all right, dear?' I asked, gently patting the grinning death's-head tattooed on his biceps. Another biker burst through the door and made for the gutter, his face blanched as white as his eyes. 'The Tube,' he moaned. Death's-Head gulped and nodded. 'Swear to God, lady, he snakes this tube up his nose and down his

throat, and then he . . . ' The pale biker flopped to his knees, gagging and retching. Death's-Head's eyes clicked up into his head. 'Oh, no,' he said. He lurched towards the kerb, belt chains jangling. I stepped inside with a spewing chorus behind me.

The joint was jammed with chic club girls, sleek club boys, and bald or bearded leather-clad biker hulks, all standing on tiptoe to peer over one another's shoulders into an open stairwell. This mismatched crowd shared a bulging of mascaraed or wind-battered eyes, a shocky looseness of their dropping jaws. They were all hanging on to something – railings, chairbacks, each other – as though they were fighting a high wind. Tinny boom-box music drummed up from the stairwell, building tension. I couldn't see what was happening down there, but the jaws of the crowd in front of me were dropping lower and lower. The music stopped. The room let out a single breath all at once and the height of the crowd dropped three sudden inches as they all plopped down off their toes. Then a voice roared up, deep and demanding, with the unmistakable vaudevillian tang of carny, of ringmaster, of Jim Rose.

Their dressing room was a wide space in the hall, three steps back under the stairs. The crowd milled woozily around asking for autographs. The Marvels were young and fresh-faced, excited and exhausted. Jim Rose himself was the size and build of a lightweight boxer. Shirtless beneath a leather vest, he was whip lean, every muscle exposed. He had cop eyes, constantly searching, and a kind of animal wariness.

He bustled around tending the props and kept his crew giggling helplessly as he regaled me with the hazards of performing at the bottom of a stairwell for a crowd looking down from above – spilt or thrown drinks, saliva dripping from gaping jaws, the threat of someone so touched by the act as to puke down on to the performer or topple over the rail and fall on to the electrocution machine. They had to drive back to Seattle that night.

When I left, the two big bikers were sitting side by side on the kerb in the rain, mopping their faces and telling each other again and again what they'd seen.

The university forbade naked flames and crotches, and various other appurtenances, in the auditorium, so the Marvels were somewhat hampered in expressing themselves. But, after the droning literary portion of the evening, Jim Rose and his Marvels stood in line before a few hundred sophisticated intellectuals and took turns making them blink and gasp. Though many a hand lifted to cover the eyes, most kept the fingers spread to peer through, and nary a scholar moved to leave. It was by far the most entertaining reading I ever gave or attended, and I've considered Jim Rose my true friend from that night forward.

Things were moving fast for the Jim Rose Circus Sideshow. Their days of appearing at private parties and openings were few. In mere weeks they were the hottest ticket in Seattle's rock clubs. At the Crocodile Club hundreds crammed in so tight they would have hyperventilated for a baroque trio. When Jim and his troupe were in full swing, the fans would squeak and scream and faint like flies, then climb one another's shoulders to see more. When it was over, the crowd crushed forward to buy souvenir T-shirts autographed on the spot by still-steaming Marvels.

There are more polished performers in the elaborate

tableaux that now pass for circuses, but none who draw their audience to greater wonder and awe, or more deeply draining delight. The gritty gift of Jim Rose is the shocking credibility of roughness. You believe it because you see it with your own eyes and feel it in your own guts, and there's nothing slick about it.

For several months, until the troupe set off on the road through Canada and eventually to tour with Lollapalooza, I took every opportunity to see their show. Jim gave me endless free passes and I enjoyed the insider feel of going backstage to visit. The show focused on geek elements modernized by imaginative technology. I considered myself far too sophisticated in carny ways to be offended, much less nauseated. But there were moments that always plunged me into a disorientating dizziness.

The show was never the same twice. Jim was constantly testing, questioning, adjusting, adding and subtracting. He tinkered endlessly with timing and revising his ringmaster patter. He tried out new acts – the rodeo rope dancer, the hula-hoop contortionist – gauging the impact of what he called 'geek relief', of the pretty versus the mind-boggling.

In our phone, tavern and green-room conversations Jim talked often about his aim to resurrect the old sideshow form. He is a fan of rash bunkum from P. T. Barnum to Howard Stern, and a scholar of fierce physical disciplines from the Hindu yogis to Fakir Musafar. He's also a cream-puff patsy in loud armour. I've seen him march into the crowd to beg, plead and finally order families to take their money back and leave before the show begins because he doesn't think small children should see it. I've seen him gravely advise a pair of reluctant grandparents to take their pre-schoolers to a Disney flick up

the street. In public he swears it's just to prevent lawsuits, but privately he confesses, 'I wouldn't let any kid of mine watch this stuff.'

The one thing I could think of to repay Jim Rose's generosity was to introduce him to my friend Melissa Rossi, the brilliantly witty writer who was the Seattle stringer for *Newsweek* magazine. When I called, Melissa informed me ominously that she had been hearing about Rose and his show for weeks. The subsequent item in *Newsweek* was the first of what became a river of national and international media coverage. She and Jim and his wife, Bebe the Circus Queen, became friends and when Jim contracted to do this book, Melissa Rossi was the collaborator he chose. But I claim the credit for giving her his phone number.

Just before he took off on the tours that would last virtually for years and take in three continents, Jim made me an offer I couldn't refuse. He would teach me to eat fire. As a stodgy, ageing desk jockey, I had read and written for years about the feats he and his Marvels performed. I had watched their acts from out front and behind the stage. I had seen them in the dressing rooms of a dozen venues preparing their gear, talking about their process, chortling over errors and accidents. Eating fire was the simplest item in their vast bag of tricks. Most of the troupe ate fire with obvious ease. It wasn't half as challenging as breathing fire, which he said I shouldn't try right away. Yes, please, I crowed. Yes. I was eager. I was confident. It would be a snap. I bragged to my friends in advance. I fantasized this new skill adding sparks to my future literary appearances.

We arranged to do it in the big green room of the Melody Ballroom following a show. Thousands crammed the

auditorium, and the show was more outrageous than ever. Big side screens and a video camera allowed even those in the seats farthest from the stage to see every detail in vivid colour and larger-than-life size. The T-shirts and posters sold by the gross. Jim ran out to count the puddles of puke leading away from the door and returned declaring the night a success.

Then it was time. The Marvels gathered around to watch. They had made me a novice's extra-small torch – a tightly wound ball of cotton thread, knotted around the end of a long wire handle. They demonstrated slowly, dipping the ball into the volatile clear fluid, shaking off the excess, lighting it, tipping back the head, opening wide. Why, I thought, it's just a burning marshmallow on a stick. The idea was to stick the ball into my mouth, flattening my tongue and breathing outwards the whole time, then close my lips around it. Cutting off the oxygen would quench the fire. Simple.

I was fascinated, cheery and cocky . . . until the flaming ball actually approached my mouth. The heat beat at my face. It was real. The flames muttered and snapped. The reek of highly refined petroleum stung my nose and the roof of my mouth. Sudden terror electrified me. I froze. This was far worse than looking down from the garage roof when your brother dares you to jump off. This was an altogether different fear than the numb anxiety of a bumpy ride in a small plane. This was sizzling, blistering, agonizing destruction. This was fire. Every cell in my body said NO! The Marvels were watching. Jim, worried and kind, was watching. I wanted to do it. I wanted to be home on the sofa watching the Weather Channel.

Gently, Jim took the torch and demonstrated again. The Marvels demonstrated. Simple. The easiest of their stunts. I

tried again. And again. First I froze when the torch was inches from my face. Then I managed to get it inside my gaping mouth but yanked it back, unable to close around it. Images of my own scorched and blackened tongue filled my head.

Finally, I managed to close my mouth around the torch, snuffing it instantly. But, despite the Marvels' many warnings, I closed too tightly around the wire handle and burned my lower lip. A tiny burn, the length of an ant, its pain quite insignificant.

I was tremendously relieved and thrilled to have managed it at all. But Jim Rose snatched the dead torch away and jumped to apply salve to my burn, gibbering apologies and cursing himself for stupidity. He was sweating and his hands were quivering. My panic and hesitation had scared him almost as badly as me.

The Marvels were gracious about my failure, and promised to give me another lesson whenever I want. So far I haven't asked. Jim gave me the torch as a souvenir. It hangs now from the ceiling of my office, a charred reminder of the real lesson that Jim and the fire taught me. I had grotesquely underestimated the raw daring and the incredible self-discipline required to learn even apparently easy stunts. My safe, distantly bookish knowledge was the worst form of ignorance, a smugness that blinded me to what the fainting fans understand far better. Now I see Jim's show through very different and far more frightened eyes. However blithe their demeanour and snappy their patter, Jim Rose and his Marvels are not like you and me.

Katherine Dunn

Enigma, Rubberman, Zen Master, Jim, Mark the Knife, Bebe, Bam Bam the Stringman, Lifto.

A FAINT IS A FALLING OVATION

I just wanted to sleep. A simple act ordinarily. But when you're wedged between a half-dozen freaks in a van without shocks, when you're smashed between swords and jars of squirming worms, in a foreign country where authorities are trying to boot you out around every bend, well, sleep is a much more difficult feat than smashing your face in glass and having people stand on your head for a living. Especially when you're wondering if you really should have convinced your circus troupe – who'd only last week been a pharmacist, dry cleaner, insurance salesman and movie projectionist – to quit their day jobs.

Not that our sub-Motel Six travelling conditions across Canada were hampering the rest of the Jim Rose Circus in their pursuit of slumber. Bebe the Circus Queen had abandoned her letter-writing and crashed out, smashing her angular face into my left shoulder. She wore the high-cheekboned look well,

but I didn't; my arm was asleep, I wished my brain would follow. Slug, the sword-swallowing insectivore, was passed out, slobbering on my right shoulder, blasting bug breath in my face every time he exhaled. Only God knew what strange insect bacteria lurked in his polymucalsaccharide droolings that were now making a big wet spot on my shirt. A clunking sound from the seat behind alerted me that Lifto's fuchsia-haired, multi-pierced head had once again collided with Matt the Tube's bald one. The Tube, his hands still clutching the gas mask that he donned whenever I smoked, jerked his head to the right, colliding with the fitful thrashing of the Human Pincushion, whose book, *Conspiracy's Greatest Hits*, tumbled into the danger zone we called the floor.

After five days on the road that area below us looked like a trough: half-eaten cans of Spaghetti Os, smashed popcorn, hairballs, Marlboro butts that had spilled from the overflowing ashtray, a used condom or two.

Hanging out with freaks can be disgusting. I'd never had to for this many days in a row.

Now they were making me sick. All the more so since they could sleep through this hell that could induce insomnia in a narcoleptic, and I couldn't.

It was May 1992 and this was our first circus tour. For the past four months the Jim Rose Circus had been a loose-knit assemblage of odd humans, who by day held real jobs, and by night took their party tricks to the stage and transformed themselves into human marvels. We were the misfits of Seattle's grunge scene, the only club act in town that would rather swallow a drumstick than pound it.

Not only did we having nothing in common with most of humanity; we really had nothing in common among ourselves

– except a desire to perform mind-boggling physical miracles in the hope of popping the audience's eyes out, and maybe making a few of them faceplant on the cold club floor. Not a lofty goal, but, given our sell-out shows in Seattle over the past few months, it seemed a potentially profitable one. Or so I'd convinced the troupe, after that phone call a few weeks before. Canada was on the line, luring us up north with the promise of international fame, adventure and Canadian coins.

Five days into it and the coins had been few. The greatest adventure so far had been watching the Human Pincushion gradually discolour – after so many shows in a row he was turning into a five-foot-nine-inch bruise. As for international fame, I wouldn't know – we piled back into our van and roared into the sleepless night long before the reviews rolled out.

Except for the press, who had swarmed us in Vancouver, and the fans, who screamed and yelled and finger-wrote graffiti on the side of our grimy van, Canada wasn't exactly rolling out the red carpet. In fact, Canada was rolling it up about the second our piece-of-shit murky-blue van came into view.

The border crossing took eight hours as guards rifled through our equipment, looking warily at the electrocution machine, strings of razor blades, jumbo-sized needles, meat skewers, a force-feeding tube. The troupe, except for Lifto's pink hair, looked wholesome enough, but immigration officers gave us the eye and the third degree as if we were a band of roving serial killers heading over the border in search of new meat.

'We're a circus, here to entertain little children,' I lied. 'Please give us back those T-shirts and maggots.'

Once we were over the border, the unwelcome-wagon treatment continued. The province of Alberta prematurely bade us *adieu*, hastily passing new laws that barred us from playing the clubs where we'd been booked. Toronto's mayor threatened to boot us out of her city before we'd even arrived. The whole tour was teetering on the brink of cancellation, and I wondered if we'd all meet back in Seattle next week, in the unemployment line.

I didn't care at that moment, though. I didn't care if the press labelled me – Jim Rose – the world's most mesmerizing circus troupe leader, I didn't care if they talked about Lifto's dick swing or the Tube's bile beer. I didn't care if we got raves or pans, or if Montreal kicked us out too. I didn't even care if the troupe disbanded at the next rest stop, smashing my dreams of reinventing the sideshow.

I just wanted to sleep. Sitting in the same place for eleven hours, suffering between wafts of Lifto's chronic farting and the Tube's smelly feet, I hadn't slept in four days, and we had three interviews and two shows that night. And everybody was snoring but me.

My eyes looked down, questioningly. My mind said no. My legs said yes. I crawled on to the floor, found a space above the one-step stairwell that we called the Donkey Cum Vat, because of the gunk and freak muck that oozed from it, and curled up like a dog.

The floor, home to many a spilled beer and Pepsi, was like a layer of rubber cement. The shocks from this level were worse, and a bump in the road reverberated through every cell in my body. I longed for something to lay my weary head on. Lifto's cowboy boot would have made a tempting pillow, but glued as I was to the floor in my curled-up position I was

unable to crawl towards it. Besides, it was too close to the Tube's malodorous feet.

It was truly a dismal moment in my career – worse than the years I'd spent professionally exterminating the creatures that Slug now swallowed for fun. And with one sharp bend in the road that low, low moment dipped lower. As the rickety van rounded the curve, the heaping ashtray perched on the seat arm above me went flying, flipping mid-air and dumping its contents on to my head.

There was only one thing to do. I flicked the ashes off my face, corralled the cigarettes into a heap, and made a small pillow of butts.

It was not the freshest-smelling bundle I've ever laid my head on, but it worked. When I next opened my eyes, two hours later, we were in Montreal and the van had stopped moving. At least it had stopped moving in a forward direction. It was, instead, rocking side to side.

I picked the pillow out of my hair, peeled my face off the floor and peered out of the smoke-clouded window. A sea of teenagers was mobbing the van. Hundreds of them were out there, screaming, 'Jim Rose! Lifto! Pincushion! Circus Queen! Tube! Hey, Slug, we brought you roadkill!'

Things were definitely looking up.

There are two quick rules of thumb a freak show uses to measure success. One is being mobbed. The second is making your fans faint. Nothing in the world is more flattering than a horizontal audience member with bubbles coming out of nose and mouth.

And the Canadians were heavy on the compliments that weekend. In Montreal we played at a nightclub we called the Electric Butt, although the actual name in French, Foufounes

Electriques, made it sound a lot classier; then again, in French 'scrotum-scratching' sounds sexy.

The Butt was the biggest, hippest and artiest club we'd ever played at that point. A sprawling multi-level number that took up most of a block, it had chain-link fences snaking through it, and spray-painted graffiti screamed from the walls in the curving halls and balconies that jutted off everywhere. A real modern-day Carnegie Hall, at least to us.

On Friday six hundred smashed into the place for our show. On Saturday we had a full house again, and turned hundreds away. The management knew we could sell out a third time, but had booked a band for the room. They frantically searched all over the city for a space. On Sunday we played the only place they could find: under a terrace, out back behind the Butt.

They hastily built us a stage in that open-aired warehouse typically used for trash storage. They stapled garbage bags over the back fence, so no one could peek in for free, and went on to staple up more, to make us garbage-bag dressing rooms. We weren't complaining: having used everything from rat-infested stairwells to PortaPottis for quick changes, a garbage-bagged backstage was nearly a step up.

But then it started raining. Pouring. A Canadian-style typhoon. And the terrace wasn't much of a shelter. It turned into Niagara Falls Jr. Water cascaded down from it, forming a small river on the stage. The club set out buckets; sandbags were in order.

The haphazardness of this outdoor show was stressing out the troupe, and some of them were hitting the bottle – moderately, of course. Since Montreal rarely enforces nudity laws, Lifto was being his typical exhibitionist self and prancing

about the stage naked, which somehow made the orange frilly-ended toothpick he'd rammed through his nose seem all the more obscene, perhaps because it clashed with his pink hair. 'Oh my God,' he wailed, his giraffe-like legs teetering in sparkly high heels as he sloshed across our makeshift stage. 'What are we going to do with the water? What's going to happen when we get to the electrocution act?'

I didn't know. One time we'd done the electrocution while the Pincushion stood in a pail of water, and it worked fine. Standing in an onstage river couldn't be that much different.

Besides, I had something else on my mind: the crowd in front of us. They were wild. There must have been some serious buzz about us all weekend because even more had turned out – and they'd obviously seen the interview taped in Vancouver and broadcast on national TV, when we dared all of Canada to bring us something that Slug wouldn't eat.

Oh, they'd brought stuff, all right. Everywhere I looked they were holding up the Kibbles 'N Bits they'd brought to feed the slugivore, waving bags of chicken gizzards, swinging rats by their tails. I made a note not to sit next to Slug on the way back. His breath would be grosser than ever.

So I'm introduced onstage in the midst of this mayhem, and this was an easy crowd to warm up – because they were already ballistic. 'We give back to you the same energy you give us,' I said into the mike, in a creepy, hypnotic way with my eyes wide open for effect. 'So I want you to scream and clap at the count of three. You, sir, get your hands out of your pockets – it's gonna hurt when you clap. Ready? One, two, motherfuckin' three.'

The response was scary. The roar made my ears ring.

These guys were wired. Crazed. Insane. Already. And Lifto's act would only rev them up more.

'And now, the most popular vulgar display since the outlawing of public hangings,' I said as Lifto staggered onstage. 'The Amazing Mr Lifto.'

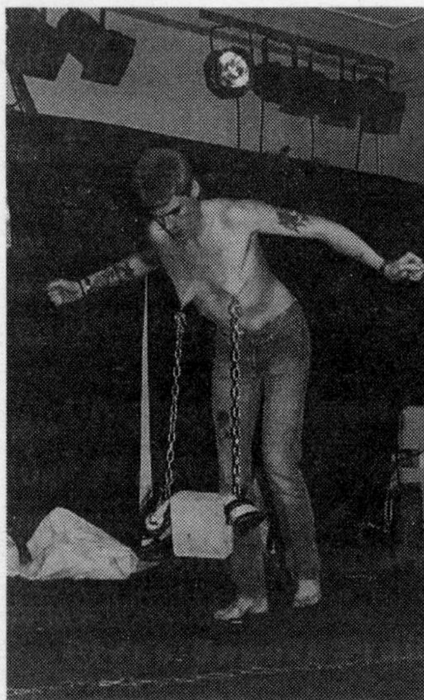

Lifto lifting a concrete block and two irons with his nipples.
Photo by Bebe Rose

Slug hit a piercing note on the keyboard as Lifto began attaching ornaments to his eleven pierced body parts. Lifto hoisted two black irons, attaching one to each of his fleshy earlobes. His ears stretched down to his shoulders. The crowd groaned.

He hooked a suitcase to his tongue. It yanked out of his mouth, stretched past his chin. The crowd screamed. He chained his nipples to a concrete block. And pulled. As if elasticized, his teats became two pointy rubber bands. The audience went berserk. 'The man,' I yelled, 'that makes Dolly Parton look flat!'

Of course, I sounded cool, calm and every bit the professional showman that I pretend to be. But between sleep deprivation and the water onstage, I was edgy. Real edgy. Delirious.

When Lifto stuck a hook through that part of him that's most a mister, I had to close my eyes. For one brief second I thought I saw him rocking in those high-heeled shoes and

feared he would do an onstage nosedive. Upon opening my eyes I was filled with relief. Lifto was still standing, his schlong stretched to the floor. Nothing out of the ordinary. 'Stretches two feet and loses nothing in girth! Just don't try this at home,' I warned the crowd. 'Go to your neighbour's house.'

The unhooked Lifto stumbled offstage, Matt the Tube sloshed on, hot water bottle in hand. He donned safety goggles, and put the bottle to his lips, as I lulled the crowd with onstage patter. 'One false move and he could blow out his lungs,' I bellowed. 'He needs your help, ladies and gentlemen. Blow, Tube, blow!!' Beads of sweat broke out on Tube's shiny head, his face turned red. 'Blow, Tube, blow!' the audience chanted. 'Blow, Tube, blow!' The red water bottle inflated to the size of a cantaloupe, a watermelon, a pregnant sheep that's ready to drop. And then – KABOOM! – it burst into douche-bag shrapnel.

The audience swarmed the stage as Slug, dressed in tuxedo, tails and tie, ran from keyboard to centre-stage spotlight, pulling handfuls of slugs, worms, crickets and maggots out of glass jars. The unfortunate creatures squirmed and recoiled as he playfully dangled them down his throat and pulled them back out.

Slug dropped one worm onstage, and it wiggled about attempting to make a last-minute escape. 'Ohhh, Slug – don't eat that one,' I cautioned. 'It's been on the floor. Probably has hair on it.' Slug smiled knowingly, picked up the worm and slid it into his mouth, along with a handful of others, whose ends dangled, swishing, from his moist lips. Gulping gleefully, he thrust a sword down his throat to push everything down.

When he pulled it out, the sword was covered with slime and goo. 'Yum,' I said, 'oesophagus gum and slug residue!

But Slug still looks hungry! Time for dessert! Who brought something to feed the insectivore?'

Like I had to ask. Dozens of fans ran to the stage, presenting him with bags and dishes heaped with fish heads, mice smashed in traps, lugie cocktails, gunk from garbage disposals, junk scraped off roads. Slug opened his mouth and polished off his treats with relish, licking his fingers with gusto, not letting on that this stuff was crossing even his line.

After that revolting spectacle we needed a vision of loveliness, and at that moment Bebe the Circus Queen appeared, her black hair pinned up loosely on her head, her black lace dress flowing behind her. 'Any time my lovely wife Bebe and I have an argument,' I said, 'I know I'm in for a hard night. Because, you see, I'm the Human Dartboard. And she throws the darts.' I ripped off my vest and held a piece of wood to my back, to avoid spinal tap. 'I'm looking for a new human dartboard,' I said to the crowd. 'The last one had a severe alcohol problem – they usually do. If you think you have what it takes to be the next goalie for the darts team, see me after the show.' That was Bebe's cue to start flinging.

Whack! The first dart landed mid-back on the right. Whack! The second hit the neck. Whack! Lower left back. Whack!

Suddenly, the promoter appeared stage right, waving his hands. I assumed he was just being friendly, notifying us that we were putting on a great show, and did my best to ignore him. But then I noticed he was having a conniption. Right in the middle of my act. 'One second, dearest!' I said to Bebe, and stomped to the side of the stage, darts bobbing from my back every step, like medals on a general.

'The flics!' moaned the promoter, frantically pulling at his

greasy blond ponytail. 'The flics! The show eez fini!' He started going off in high-speed French, and I pulled over Bebe, who grew up in France, for a translation. Turns out that neighbours were complaining about the ruckus and the ear-splitting noise coming from the show. The cops were searching the block-long building, trying to discover the source. 'When zey find you back ere, it eez all over!' the promoter wailed.

I looked out at the mob, standing there screaming in the rain, and thought, Oh God. If we shut down this show, they're going to freak. They're going to riot. They're going to get their money refunded, and we'll have done this hell show for nothing – and the final use for those damn garbage bags will be to haul out our corpses.

So I stepped up to the mike, wondering all the while how the *Seattle Times* would write up my obituary. 'Ladies and gentlemen,' I began warily in a hushed tone, 'don't shoot the messenger. But we might have to shut down this show. The police are in the area, and if they find out we're here, it's all over.' The audience immediately started booing and hissing and shuffling around in that nervous way cattle do before a stampede. 'But with your help we can remedy this situation,' I continued, talking off the top of my head. 'We can hide from them. They won't even know we're here . . . if we do a whisper show.'

Now, I was talking to a crowd of young hellions, punks, cowboys and heavy-metal guys, not exactly your low-decibel sort. Plus their adrenalin was surging. There was that madness in their eyes that made it obvious they were oblivious to reason. And we'd driven them to that state; it was up to me to unwind them and, frankly, I wasn't sure how to.

'That's right, a whisper show,' I said very quietly in the

hope of inducing a collective trance state. 'So nobody screams and nobody yells. Instead, whenever you see something you like, you just go, Shhhh!'

Then a weird thing happened. The room actually went silent, as if our fans had been megadosed with Valium. And then it started sounding like a cross between a snake pit and a roomful of librarians, as the masses practised their Shhhs.

Amid this stillness the Human Pincushion strode out, his dark hair pulled back, a cape around his shoulder, his look stoic. He dropped the cape, exposing his bare torso and legs – which were festooned with forty hatpins and meat skewers. He looked like a voodoo-doll nightmare. Waves of 'Shhh, shhh' rolled across the crowd. He slid three more pins through one cheek and out the other. 'Shhhhh! Shhhhh!'

'And to every one of these hatpins and skewers, we've attached a light bulb,' I whispered. 'Put your arms in the air, ladies and gentlemen, because here's our electric Jesus.' I switched on the copper generator that stood a few feet away from the Pincushion. Lightning bolts charged out, striking the pins and illuminating the red and green bulbs.

That's standard procedure. But this time something was wrong. Water must have got into the generator. The bulbs were burning brighter than ever before. The bolts were huge. Our electric Jesus was getting far too much juice. And the Pincushion, the man who never winces, had a look of sheer terror in his eyes, which were bulging out of his head.

And then something stranger happened. The Pincushion does not bleed. I sometimes wonder if the guy really has blood in his body. I got my answer that night. His heart must have tweaked from his standing in water being zapped with excessively high voltage. Because suddenly the Human

Pincushion not only began to bleed, he started to gush. Every time his heart beat, blood spurted out a few feet – from forty holes across his body. He was a fucking geyser.

'SHHHHHH!' The crowd was going nuts. 'SHHHHH! SHHHHH!' They were loving it. The whole room was wave after wave of 'SHHHH!' And when I looked out over the masses, I saw a strange downward movement. One by one they were faceplanting. Like dominoes. Faint, faint, faint. 'SHHHHHHHHH! SHHHHHHH! SHHHHHH!' About every tenth person was down. We were getting falling ovations everywhere. There must have been a hundred by then, and every time they breathed, bubbles came from nose and mouth, as their significant others patted them down with wet rags.

The Pincushion was helped off the stage and given towels to aid the coagulation. His recuperative abilities amaze me to this day.

In the midst of the frenzy Matt the Tube returned to the stage – his force-feeding tube in hand. He looked like Mr Clean – that no-nonsense, bald, cross-armed giant who flies off floor-detergent bottles in TV ads. Handing me a large clear cylinder with a tube attached to it, he proceeded to thread the plastic tube forcefully up his right nostril. 'Watch him snake seven feet of tubing into his stomach, via the nose,' I murmured to the crowd. Once the tube had been shoved down his oesophagus and was eeling around in the bottom of his stomach, he cracked open a dozen eggs, poured in ketchup, mustard, chocolate syrup, a quart of Miller beer. He then affixed a plunger atop the cylinder, turning it into a pump. I hooked the pump under my arm and pushed – forcing the gooey concoction into his stomach, until nothing of his liquid diet remained. 'A complete tastebud bypass,' I said. 'This is a

man who loves to get drunk, but he hates the taste of beer.' The audience was aghast. 'Miller beer – tastes great or less filling? The scientist in me has got to know.' And then I pulled the plunger up, creating a vacuum; the chartreuse bile was sucked back up into the cylinder. 'We always know what the Tube had for dinner,' I said. 'Tonight it looks like tacos and *escargots*.'

I saw that queasy swaying and the Shhhs turned to Oh nooos as he started to drink it. 'It's that after-aftertaste you've got to worry about,' I said. 'You would think it tastes like shit, he only wishes it was.' The faints were multiplying like amoebas. It was becoming a floor show. The bubbles on the noses and mouths were now coming from a deeper part of the anatomy and were a slightly different colour. Since the first fainters were up front, we started piling them onstage rather than push through the crowd. But then more and more were going horizontal. Everywhere faint, faint, faint, followed by 'SHHHHHH! SHHHHH! SHHHHH!' So many had fallen victim to queasiness that there wasn't room left on the stage for them. The fainters – there must have been two hundred by then – were piling up. The remaining bystanders and queasy teeterers swayed and stumbled, leaving no room for the horizontally inclined. We had to designate an official 'fainters' corner'. Security men joined in the bouncers' troupes and began passing bodies overhead. Slug played a funeral dirge. The spotlight slipped from the stage – and beamed on the procession.

I was suddenly reminded of the Ayatollah Khomeini. Remember when the old man finally died, and they carried his casket through the street but then it tipped over and his dead-as-a-doornail corpse came flying out?

When I looked out over the crowd I was seeing the same

thing. No matter how hard everyone tried to make this an organized procession, every so often one of the fainters would tip over and drop into the audience. Every time another body was dropped, the crowd erupted like at a soccer game.

The crowd was in a frenzy. SHHHHHH! SHHHHHHH! SHHHHHHHH! I didn't know how we could keep a lid on this pressure cooker.

Just then the promoter returned, yelling about the 'the flics' again. This time he had good news: the cops were gone.

So I went back to the mike, and screamed. 'LET'S FINISH THIS SHOW AND FINISH IT RIGHT.' The audience began chanting at the top of their lungs, 'Throw your ass in the glass.'

I walked to the mountain of fifty broken bottles and complied. 'Montreal, this is how I shave!' I bellowed, burying my face in the shards of glass, while a burly cowboy stomped on my head.

Cheers resounded throughout the space. My head still in glass, I wearily mumbled into the mike, 'It's the lowest form of entertainment! Thank you for coming, get the fuck off my head!'

When we had piled the swords, the electrocution machine and the jars of slugs back into the van, as we lugged our weary bodies back into the seats, I didn't know that we'd be written up in *Newsweek* within twenty-four hours, that we'd be on *Sally Jessy Raphael* within a week, that we'd be booked with Lollapalooza in a matter of days. I had only one thought: I just wanted to sleep. And I'd never learn how to do it sitting wedged between freaks. I vowed this was our last van ride. Next tour we'd have a bus.

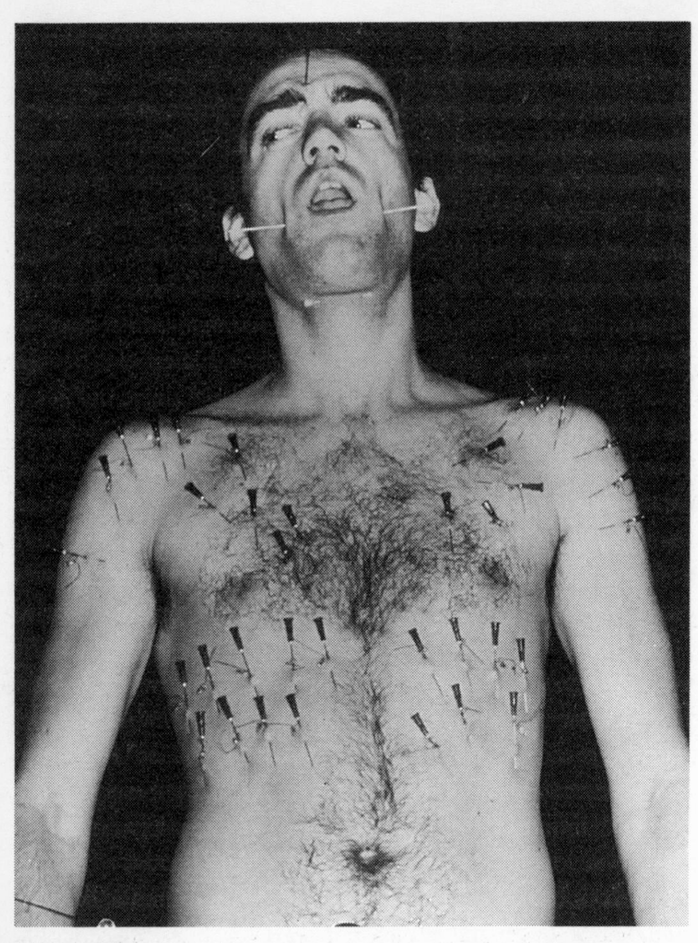

Pincushion.
Photo by Alison Braun

FREAK LIKE ME

Today, I play a freak on TV. But not long ago I really was one. My mothers looked like former beauty queens, and my fathers looked like Johnny Carsons. Or so it seemed to me, because I was born with the world's most fascinating nose. A nose so intriguing, my eyes couldn't stop looking at it. Which is to say, in the optical department, I was cross-eyed.

My nose was the precipice from which I saw the fuzzy world – double. Every image before me, except for that nose, came complete with a Siamese twin: two grilled-cheese sandwiches on the Flintstones plates before me, two fingers wagging at me, two Gingers on the two TV screens. Two sets of crossed eyes staring back at me in the mirror, making me feel like a freak.

It was an affliction that had skipped a generation, having been handed on like fine china by my grandmother Ruby Rose. 'Jimmy,' my mother would say, shoving me towards the smell of lavender and the soft grandmotherly face, 'kiss Grandma on the nose – so she can see you.' Meanwhile, I was having a hard time figuring out the precise location of

Grandma's nose, which, like the rest of the world, was a double image.

My mother, a knockout who subscribed to the pre-Virginia Slims outlook, and my dad, a former military man, had both grown up in McGehee, Arkansas, a small town of three thousand where most of the names were Rose or McGehee. When they travelled across Arizona in the early years of their marriage, the south-west's red sunsets, the desert landscape and dry, dusty air seemed so exotic that it might as well have been Africa. They pulled into a gas station, where Dad got a fill-up, and minutes later a job, and they stayed.

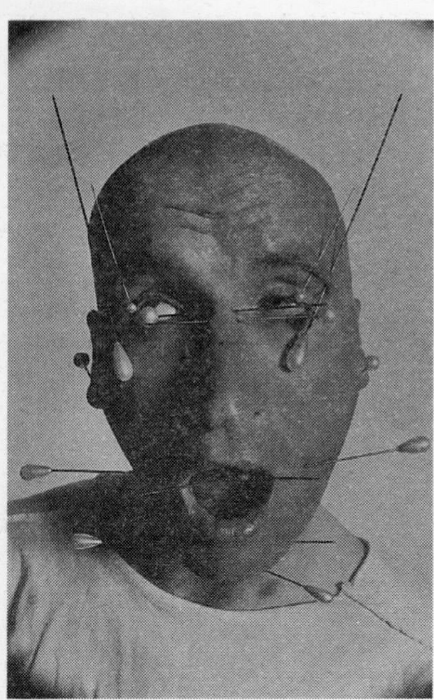

Scottish Pincushion.
Photo by Jim Rose

Phoenix was an unruly boomtown back then in the early 60s, thanks to doctors nationwide and Dristan commercials which suggested that, to do your sinuses a favour, move to Arizona. Waves of old people and the respiratorially challenged packed up their bags and wheezed into town, where hastily erected tract houses sprawled across the flood-prone flatlands. Palm trees were shipped in from California to

line the highways and give the town even more of a tropical feel, and Phoenix quickly became a land of continuous strip malls, punctuated by golf courses and pools.

Given the geriatric population, the kids, even the little kids, in Phoenix had seen a lot: a cane, a wheelchair, a colostomy bag or two. But crossed eyes, my cross to bear – now those were a rarity. I might as well have had two heads, with the reaction I triggered. Their double-takes looked quadruple to me. My peers would take one glance, start screaming and bolt. Little children pointed at me and clung to their mother's skirts, sobbing. Other people *tsked, tsked* me; big kids kicked me around. I was a monster. And I wasn't alone for long.

I remember the horror I felt at the age of three when my brother, Willy, was born. A premature baby, he was so tiny he could fit in a shoebox. His weight escapes me, but his length was a men's size seven. When little Willy opened his eyes and gazed up at my parents and me, he saw twelve eyes looking back at him, looking at his nose. He had the same fascinating Ruby Rose nose. He, too, was crossed.

I didn't want to be in his shoebox, but I was. My sister, born the previous year, was in it as well. Family photos were a treat: distant relatives and faraway friends who received our Christmas photo-postcards thought we were clowning around, making funny faces for the camera each and every year.

My youngest sister was the only one of us born with something resembling straightforward eyes. Even as a toddler she'd always find the golden egg in the Easter-egg hunts; the competition was scarcely fierce; the rest of us spent our time running into each other.

In later years I learned that in a certain African tribe, the

men line up and bare their teeth and cross their eyes as a ritual of courtship – and whoever crosses his eyes the best snags the princess. In western Europe, however, crossed eyes were considered the evil eye, and anyone who had them was cursed.

My peers in kindergarten and first grade were clearly of European descent. They made me feel cursed. Hell, I *was* cursed. They pointed at me, called me names, beat me up any time I looked in their direction.

One time in the hallway a kid bumped into me, sending my Jetsons lunchbox flying. 'Hey,' I snarled, 'look where you're going!'

'Hey,' he snarled back, 'go where you're looking.'

I was tormented hourly, being reminded that I was a weirdo by at least fifty kids a day. Sensing my growing alienation, my father would often take me fishing out in the country, and there, gazing over the lakes and the fields, I became two with nature.

From age three on I wore a pair of heavy glasses so thick I could see gnats mating on Pluto. The glasses didn't help, doing little more than make my ears ache and giving the kids more abuse ammunition. I was the four-eyed cross-eyed. I was a mess.

But one balmy spring night when I was in first grade, and crying over my plates of dinners, my parents dished me a portion of really good news. 'Jimmy,' Mom said in that way she used when presenting a birthday present, 'we're going to get you a special operation for your eyes.'

Yippee! A kid was never so happy knowing he'd be going to the hospital. Yahoo! A special operation to uncross my eyes. That news was better than Christmas and Easter

combined. Alas, the big day was two months away.

The countdown began immediately – and I alerted my classmates hourly how many days it would be before I had straight-looking eyes too, and that they better watch out when I could see straight. My first thought every morning, my last every night, was my upcoming uncrossing. I marked the dates off the calendars with thick red crayons and ridiculous glee.

And though hospitals are traumatic for most kids, my operation seemed so magical that the antiseptic land of tubes, masks and knives was like Disneyland with lots of nurses. I didn't care that they poked my arms and prodded everywhere and took my temperature in a different way than Mom did at home; they were going to give me new, normal eyes.

When I came out, my eyes swathed in gauze, I looked like a mummified mole, or so I was told, being chided, 'Mr Mole, come out of your hole!' everywhere I went. When taunted, I swapped sarcasms with confidence, reminding everyone that, when my bandage came off, with my brand-new eyes I was gonna kick their ass, because I'd be able to see it. Willy guided me around that whole summer, in a classic case of the cross-eyed leading the blind. It seemed worth it, though – a summer of hell wasn't much to pay for a future of normality. For months my eyes remained bandaged, and I lived for the day that I could see just like a regular kid.

Finally, the week before school, the gauze was ripped off. And I looked up to see my parents and the doctors looking back at me, looking at my fascinating Ruby Rose nose. My eyes, the bane of my life, were still crossed. I was devastated.

That year – second grade – was the worst. I won the Reading Achievement award for reading the most books, simply because I was trying to hide behind pages. Most of the

time I was just a quivering wimpy heap, spending hours with my head bent on the desk, crying my little crossed eyes out; at the end of the day crooked salt trails streaked across my desk, making one big X. Life was miserable, it sucked, I wanted to hide behind sunglasses for the rest of my life – which, given the frequency I was getting beaten up, looked like it would be short.

But that summer two important things happened. I made my first escape, and found the power of mud.

I sometimes tell people that my first getaway stunt was gnawing through the umbilical cord. In fact, my first escape was prompted not by the beckoning birth canal but by *The Fugitive*. Being not only four-eyed and crossed but small and spindly as well, I was the designated runt of our neighbourhood. When it came time to line up to be cowboys and Indians, not only was I skipped over for cowboy, I was the scum of the Indians – the one who was forked over as hostage and tied up. Often and with vigour.

I didn't even need a feather or a band, all I needed was to walk out of my screen door. Every day when it slammed behind me I'd think, I'm not going to get tied up today, and every night, as I stood roped against the telephone pole waiting for my parents to retrieve me, I cursed the universe for having made me such an easy target.

One night, as I stood abandoned once again by the kids, even my parents forgot to untie me for hours. That night I missed not only dinner but *The Fugitive* – the episode where he finally found the one-armed man. The television event of the year. Hungry, thirsty and depressed, because I'd been waiting half my life for that very show, I vowed it would never happen again. And that night, I sneaked up to the attic and found an

old magic book and turned directly to the chapter on escapes.

The next day, when the cowboys wound the rope around me, I kept my arms braced along my sides – and had a full sail of wind in my lungs. Ditched again, I exhaled and wedged my arms towards my stomach, giving myself the slack to slither out.

Moments later the Indian owl hoot went out – and the kids were shocked and amazed, wondering how the little cross-eyed loser had rejoined the tribe so swiftly.

From then on I would do anything to shock and amaze my peers.

My dad, the best storyteller around, taught me the art of spinning a tale; skilled with sleight of hand, he shared the secrets of card tricks, and how to make quarters or saltshakers disappear, skills that guaranteed my presence at all birthday parties. Believing the urban legend that a canine's mouth is cleaner than a human's, I'd lie on the floor, pour milk in my mouth and let a dog lap it up. I'd put on dramatic escape stunts, daring people to tie me up. I'd do anything, and everything, to divert onlookers' eyes from mine.

Including slather myself with mud. There was a mud pit on the side of our house for a month or so every year. Each fall during the famous Arizona Indian summer, violent storms would roll in – and Phoenix was not a city that understood the concept of drainage. Every year the flat city would be flooded, and the water went up to our knees. We'd take plastic boats and sail around the neighbourhood. Imagine a little Venice with 7-Elevens everywhere, ugly tract housing and little kids rowing around in plastic boats, and that was the Phoenix of my childhood in the fall.

When the storms finally rolled back, there were giant mud pits everywhere. That year I caked myself with the stuff, and discovered an amazing thing: mud is empowering. When you're covered in it, nobody knows the colour of your skin or your hair, they can't tell what type of shoes you're wearing. All they know is that you're muddy, and it's contagious.

Mud is truly the great equalizer. It doesn't matter how tall or old you are; if you are walking down the street, people take one look at the brown ooze on your two feet and run. You can go up to a huge guy and call him a motherfucker and he's not gonna touch you, because he doesn't want to become a muddy fucker. You could terrorize young and old alike. People seemed to run faster from me, though, because all they could see was my crossed eyes gazing out from the brown goo.

Granted, after a month the novelty wore off. But discovering mud turned things around. I was no longer a victim; I was a force to be reckoned with. Instead of shying away from attention I learned how to walk in a door and make myself an event. I knew how to amuse peers and transform hostile energy, and I hadn't even read a self-help book.

For the next three years I was a wild kid, revelling in my new hyper, ultra-outgoing personality. I was the home-room jester, the playground leader, the one who led the lunch-room rebellions. I was a magician. And I was a salesman – after I figured out the secret of making X-ray glasses. You know the type: special glasses with a spiral in the lens that were advertised in the back of comic books and *Boys' Life* magazine with the promise you could see through skin and clothes.

From the second I saw that ad, I started saving for the device that would allow me to see what lurked beneath school

clothes and bathing suits and the teacher's bra. Impatient at the slow savings proceedings, I brought in a pal, Casey Bartlett, to co-finance the venture by helping me find money under the bleachers after the Little League games.

We waited for weeks for the UPS box to arrive. Once the box came I tore it open, tried the glasses on, and discovered they work by giving everything a fuzzy outline. They were such a disappointment that I ripped them apart before I ever gave Casey a chance to try them.

The magical effect – the way everything looked eerie through them, like you could see bones through skin and clothes – was made possible by a feather. A stupid feather. When light filtered through it, the result was the X-ray glow. Nothing particularly cool or high-tech. And I realized I'd stumbled on an important discovery.

I hit the park that day and scooped up a pillowcase-worth of pigeon feathers, and through the night I glued them between two index cards and punched a hole in the centre. And for the next few weeks you couldn't walk through a lunch room without every kid staring at you through a hole in an index card.

Charging 50¢ a pop, I sold dozens a day. My sales secret: I'd let the kids preview the X-ray cards looking at the bones in their hands, but if they wanted to see through clothes they had to buy it.

I was still cross-eyed, but at last I had friends – and the cowboys didn't even bother tying me up. Meanwhile my father had rounded up the parents and formed a Little League baseball team. He volunteered hours and hours each week, finding advertisers for the fences, building booths, coaching the team, and even being the father who had balls thrown at

him and fell into the dunk tank at the pre-season fund-raiser fair. For his volunteer hours he asked only one thing: that his shrimpy son be tolerated on the team.

So for a few summers I played baseball – until he stepped down as coach. I rarely saw the dirt of second base, but the three times I managed to hit the ball, it was a World Series event for me.

The summer before sixth grade I had another operation. This one took. When I walked into school that year, I was normal. For the first time in my life I was just like the other kids – except I could perform magic tricks. And by then I was a ham.

I quickly reaped the benefits of having both eyes facing in the same direction. My class elected me to student council, where my main responsibilities were overseeing the pop machine and the Christmas party.

And that year I wrote a play in a weekend that resulted in my teachers telling my parents that I was 'gifted' and 'had talent'. My true talent was stenography. Because my play was a rip-off right down to the title – *Rowen and Martin's Laugh-In* – and I had lifted the jokes directly from the show. Teachers loved it, and kids didn't mind it because watching a stupid play beat English and maths – and my home-room colleagues and I travelled for months performing my plagiarized play for schools all over Arizona.

Recognizing my initiative, the school offered me a deal for the second half of the year. I arranged it so I could skip all my classes and write another play. The only problem was I didn't bother to find another show to rip off. I called in my friends and discussed the new concept: cops and robbers.

We spent the rest of the year shooting each other, rolling

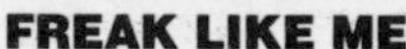

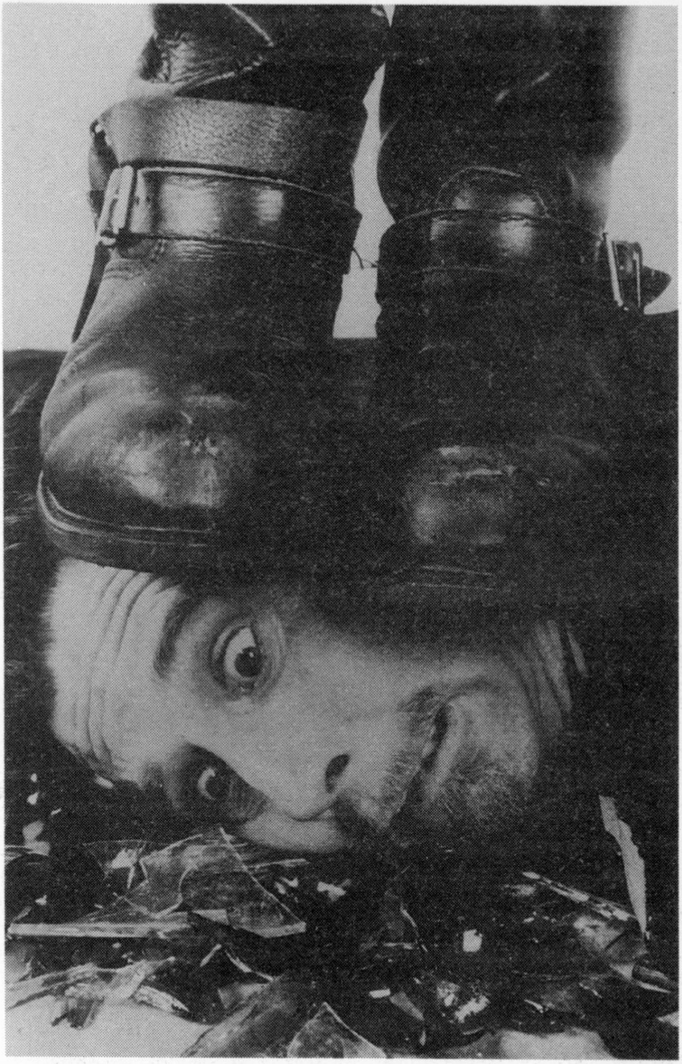

Feet on Jim in glass.
Photo by Alison Braun

around from ketchup-stain wounds, hiding in closets, popping up and blasting off cap guns. And the coolest thing was we were the only kids in school who were allowed to shoot cap guns, because we were writing a play, and sound effects are an integral part of story development. Throughout the year I was hit many times, but ink never hit the page.

That summer I was hanging out with a bunch of neighbour hoodlums who'd steal their parents' cigarettes and bottles of booze and sit around for hours blasting Black Sabbath, Alice Cooper and the Who. Later, we'd fill the bottles up with coloured water and return them to the shelves. I will never forget my friend's father bragging about the two fifths of whiskey he'd polished off the night before. In early August we jumped the fence while the Arizona State Fair was setting up at the fairground – and hustled ourselves jobs hawking soft drinks. It turned into a career: we worked at the fair for two weeks every summer all through junior high. Every year the vendor promised us a stuffed animal at the end of the two-week run, and every year we never got it. But every year we stole enough to make it worth our while.

Besides, it was educational – far more so than running around playing cops and robbers. I was mesmerized listening to the barkers verbally lassoing crowds for the sideshows with their hypnotic tape loops. 'Big Bertha,' they'd yell, 'she's big, she's fat, she's happy – ha ha ha. Takes six guys to hug her and a box car to lug her. Big Bertha, she's big, she's fat, she's happy, ha ha ha . . . ' Or, 'See, right before your very eyes, a horse smaller than a dog, a horse found in the Grand Canyon of Tucson, Arizona, a horse that stands less than two feet tall, a horse smaller than a dog!' That one cracked me up the most, because, being from Arizona, I knew

the Grand Canyon wasn't in Tucson.

I was always looking but never saw anything rigged; but I did learn the origin of the term 'easy mark'. There was always some drunk trying to impress his girlfriend, who would toss out $50 trying to win a stuffed bear that only cost 50¢. And whenever those suckers tossed out wads of money and lost a bunch of games, the guy running the outfit would pat him on the back and say, 'Hey, pal, better luck next time.' Unbeknown to the loser the comforting hand that patted was covered in chalk, clearly marking the loser's back to other barkers.

But the best thing about being a vendor was that I had the backstage view of the circus and its sideshows, freak shows and daredevil stunt acts. I watched the same shows from the front; then I watched them from backstage the next day, all the while studying the acts. I'd been to circuses; they were duds, nothing more than sequinned pageantry. This was the real thing.

Inside those side tents there were guys climbing barefoot up ladders of razor-sharp swords, guys walking across sizzling hot coals. There were sword swallowers, fire eaters, a guy who extinguished a blowtorch with his mouth, the Iron Tongue who could lift weights with his organ of taste, and motorcycle daredevils who flew their roaring bikes over ten cars. It all gave me a jolt – that edge-of-the-seat feeling that makes you feel like you're simultaneously going to puke and pee.

With the same zeal I'd once applied to ripping apart X-ray glasses, I became obsessed with looking for what gave people jolts. Before long I'd noticed one common denominator among all the shows: the jolt was rooted in fear and rebellion against moms. The stunts I was seeing were exactly the things

mothers across the world were telling their children never to do. Every time someone watched a guy setting his mouth on fire or ramming a sword down his throat, the exhilarating forbidden zone in the brain was lit.

After shows I hung around with the sweaty performers in their trailers out back, fetching them Cokes. Most of the human marvels, daredevils and stuntpeople had actually been born normal – more normal than I'd been – and had trained and transformed their bodies for years. They wouldn't tell me exactly how they'd done it, always saying, 'Kid, don't be like me, this is no way to make a living,' but I was determined to find out some day. Seeing my fascination, they began giving me photos from their collections – and I started a scrapbook of old-time pincushions and rubbermen, nature's freaks and human marvels. It had all started with those who weren't born normal; they were the most revered.

In the meantime there was one thing I could easily imitate: the carny's patter and the ability to reel people in by lulling them with his voice. It was a skill I constantly practised – whether talking to girls on the phone or telling ghost stories around the campfire. 'When Bill and Samantha woke up that morning,' I'd say, taking a drag off a cigarette stolen from somebody's mom,' the house seemed normal. At first. But then . . . '

The skill of verbal cajoling came in handy in high school, where I was a chameleon. By then my dad had traded in the gas-station job to become a real-estate assessor, and we'd moved to the wealthiest part of town – the only section of flat Phoenix upon which budded a hill. Granted, our house was on the lowest corner lot of that bud, and our pool wasn't Olympic-sized, but at least this pool was actually in the

ground, and not full of mud.

So when I started school, all my classmates were wealthy, and I quickly learned how to blend in. You want a green suit, I got a green suit. I'd learn the survival rule of the slickest.

Some nights I hung out with the rich neighbour hoodlums, trashing golf courses. Sometimes I hung out with the artist and theatre crowds. In some schools, theatre types are synonymous with nerds; at Arcadia, a culturally refined school, being an actor was cool.

I landed the first part I auditioned for – Walter Mitty in *Thurber's Carnival*. Mitty is a dorky little guy who in his fantasies transforms himself into a super-hero. I didn't need years of method acting for that part; it was my childhood story.

And the stage – well, being up there, peering out at the audience, provided every bit of the edge-of-the-seat jolt those motorcycle stunts used to give me. Besides, there was no more effective way to grab attention than to stand upon a stage. Except, that is, to run the intercom system.

'Uncle Meat was in the Basement . . . ' Those were the opening words of a tribute to Frank Zappa that ultimately put the intercom mike in my hand. Because with that humorous spoken-word piece I snagged a prize for a spoken-word competition, and became the voice of Arcadia High School. The wake-up call, the voice that boomed across loud-speakers far and wide, with the Daily Bulletin.

Every morning, instead of checking into home room, I strode into the office, pushing past the kids lined up with notes and kids who'd had their books stolen. And there behind the front desk, handily out of sight of the principal's office, was my communications kingdom: the intercom machine. A hefty metal cabinet as big as a closet, it had a microphone the size

of a shoulder and more knobs than a French tickler. I could pick and choose what news to broadcast, shuffling through the two inches of handwritten press releases. 'Good-morning, fellow-Arcadians. This is Jim Rose,' I said, emphasizing my name so it was branded into their minds, 'with the Daily Bulletin. The Smegma Club, I mean Sigma Club, will hold a meeting after school tomorrow, and bland practise will commence at three p.m. sharp. Et cetera, et cetera, you're giving me an et cetera headache.'

And then, after starting the school day for thousands, I'd sign off and slip off to the john for a smoke.

By then I loved school. I had the system rigged. My teachers were convinced I could be a professional performer, so they'd let me slide by with 'independent studies', requiring that I give one presentation per class per term. And I spent hours devising new gags for my personal three-minute morning zoo radio show. Well, it was three minutes initially. But one day, when I was fooling around with the knobs at Intercom Central, I inadvertently tuned in to the teachers' lounge. After listening for a few days I'd discovered they were playing poker.

After that I got seven minutes' airtime. I pulled in my pals, and we began doing character sketches and jokes. The favourite was 'Uncle Jaime'.

Dave Albert, a cynical, plump Jewish boy, would sidle up to the mike and put on his whiniest Yiddish accent. 'This is Uncle Hymie, critic at large,' he'd say, sounding like a haemorrhoid-suffering sixty-year-old. 'What would you like me to criticize?' He'd then go on criticizing everything from the architecture of lockers to big hair to his date that weekend. For the national anthem we'd blast Hendrix's version of

'The Star-Spangled Banner'.

I promoted myself incessantly for the upcoming senior council elections. To ensure victory I handed out roses to all of the girls – roses that I'd spent the dawn snipping from neighbours' bushes. Not a rosebush for two miles wasn't defrocked.

My senior year rocked. Student-council representative, Voice Behind the Intercom, actor, writer, entertainer. Granted, girls weren't knocking each other down to go out with me, but I was none the less popular; when I volunteered at the kissing booth at the Valentine's dance, my mouth, multicoloured with assorted shades of lip gloss, was bruised.

And my gang knew how to party. Wild weekends were the rule. By day it was proper poolside society; by night it was golf-course hooliganism, when we transformed nearby links into party centres, throwing huge bashes that hundreds crashed. Golf courses were fertile grounds for hours of entertainment.

Sprinklers became deadly weapons when they came into our hands, as we hosed down everyone who came near. We'd slide across freshly watered greens on skimboards; young lovers traipsed hand in hand to make out in the sandtrap, their moaning heard above the steady *tch, tch, tch* of the sprinklers, and their groaning even louder once we'd drenched them. And every night we made the golf carts our personal bumper cars, driving them about for hours; as a grand finale we always raced them into the pond. We trashed courses by the dozen, but there were so many, the cops never knew where we'd strike next.

One weekend my buddies and I piled into one of those hand-me-down-from-executive-Dad cars and headed to California – with two goals in mind, Disneyland and the San

Diego Zoo. Being impulsive, non-pragmatic sorts, we had about twenty dollars between us, but we compensated by creative problem-solving. In Arizona they'd just introduced self-service gas stations, and hadn't quite worked out the bugs in the system – so that you could pump gas before the person in front of you had paid. And we took full advantage of their flaws, by filling the car up and then starting the pumping routine over – and the second time only pumping in one dollar's worth. The cashier would look only at the most recent amount, and we'd fork over the dollar, having filled up the tank.

In California, however, they were wise to such scams. To set the gas tank back to zero required either paying first or setting the meter back with needle-nose pliers. Of course, we'd filled up the tank before discovering this snag. So we quickly threw up the hood, donned looks of distress, borrowed the pliers from the station, clicked the pump back to zero using their tool, and pumped in the routine dollar of gas. Keeping the pliers for future use, we plunked down the dollar and roared off.

We were hellions that trip: at Disneyland we skirted admission by climbing the fences and jumping on to the top of dog kennels, the dogs making such a racket that they covered up the sound of our steps on the metal roof; by the time security tuned in, we were riding on top of the kiddie train to our salvation, waving at the guys with walkie-talkies as we chugged away. And then we did it again for the next three days. At the San Diego Zoo the walls were even higher, requiring that we not only climb up, but down the other side, since they were too high to jump. Midway down the other side, as we were clinging to the metal, we looked up to see a tour bus, with the

guide pointing our way. 'Ladies and gentlemen,' he said, 'the most dangerous species of them all: the American teenager.'

Our shortage of money required frequent dining and dashing. One night at a Denny's I acted like I was going to the cigarette machine by the door and slipped out instead, and hid behind some cars in the lot, stranding my friend Mark at the counter. A few minutes later he came running out with an old-lady waitress at his heels. He was so drunk, she actually tackled him. While they were scuffling on the ground, he started to throw up all over her. The disgusting distraction afforded him the opportunity to flee. Upon seeing that she'd given up pursuit, Mark turned around and bellowed, 'You can't bust me now, you're wearing all the evidence.'

We didn't just strike out against establishments and authorities; being young dumbfucks, we were always pulling pranks on each other. One Hallowe'en Mark talked me into wearing a mask and a raincoat – and nothing underneath – knocking on his door and flashing his girlfriend. Of course I declined the dare, but he talked me into it. 'It'll be hilarious,' he assured me.

I knocked on the door, said, 'Trick or treat,' and she said, 'Boy, they're getting big this year.' I countered, 'You ain't seen nothing yet,' and then ripped open the raincoat and flashed. She opened the door wider, and all my friends stood there, applauding.

I could think of nothing but revenge. So I took out an ad on 26 December in the local paper saying, 'I'll pay $5 each for your used Christmas trees!!!' and listed Mark's address.

Trucks and vans and troops of Boy Scouts showed up at the door, furious when they learned they'd have to haul their

trees back. Things got so bad the family finally went on a vacation – till Arbor Day, I believe – leaving a note tacked to the door, explaining it was all just a horrible prank. When they got back, trees were everywhere: livid haulers dumped them across the driveway, tossed them into high piles in the back yard, wedged them in windows and even pitched them on top of the roof.

He got me back a week later, by mailing a huge box of rocks, CoD.

In short, life was a huge party, a twenty-four-hour-a-day scream. Until I smacked into the real world.

Bebe topless and about to be electrocuted.

When I think of my life post-high school, 'floundering' is a word that comes to mind; 'terminally depressed' are two

others. I enrolled in junior college, studied business, dropped out within a quarter. I was a car salesman, a telemarketer, an exterminator, a car salesman again. My commissions were good, my mood foul. Nothing jolted me. I was unnerved, unfocused, unwound. A spring with the coils screwed up. I was more hopeless than the little loser kid with crossed eyes.

At least I had a girlfriend, though it's a mystery now why a chronic over-achiever like her would have hung out with a walking question mark like me. She was accepted to law school at Georgetown; her siblings were all doctors, so was her father. I wasn't exactly stacking up to her family tradition. Careerwise, I was in a permanent sandtrap. So with nothing to anchor me I followed her east, not having the slightest clue what to do with the remainder of my life.

This was all before I realized that only art was going to make me happy.

Jim Rose.
Photo by David Harradine

BUGBOY GOES ABROAD

ashington, DC. For an untravelled Phoenician like me it sounded as exotic as Jupiter. Every blade of grass, every crack in the sidewalk, stepped on by our country's great men. The prestigious monuments and buildings that I'd seen only in textbooks. The pulsating power centre where vastly important decisions were made every second.

Just being out of Arizona was a jolt. And in DC my love of history and politicking would finally find a home. The air was charged. My mood was high. And I loved Georgetown, where we'd rented a lovely little duplex, in an area of gorgeous old homes, tree-lined streets and yuppie restaurants.

When we went out that first day, I immediately descended from Jupiter. Frankly, the monument tour was a huge disappointment: all the memorials looked better on postcards. The second day, I hit earth when I realized that my jobs in politics would be volunteer. And my third day I nearly went

subterranean, when I stepped off the beaten path and noticed that if you walk outside that trail you will be killed. They'll not only take your money, they'll take your rings, your necklace and your liver to sell.

DC had it all, including the highest murder rate in the country, which made the denizens incredibly uptight. Everyone darted about furtively, their face stuck on their neck at ninety degrees, permaglancing over their shoulder. But you not only had to guard your ass on the street; I quickly learned you had to watch it socially and politically as well. Because people are desperate in DC. They'd kick the gold fillings out of their mother's mouth to score drugs – or ensure election victory.

Of course, I didn't know that at first. The novelty of the city lured me in, initially. I grasped for the power vibe in the air – and landed a job as a cog in the volunteer machine. My life was schmoozing at parties, shaking hands at conventions, working the phones with surveys and reminders to vote, selling a name, an image, an important ideological message.

Politics, I quickly discovered, is the worst sales job – you sweat, you hustle, you give up all your free time, your face is flattened by slamming doors – and you don't get a salary, a commission, or even a thank-you note. But, worse, even if your candidate wins you ultimately lose, because the politicos you're selling are usually the slimiest creatures to ascend from the muck of creation. Candidates are far too often little more than walking ectoplasm, missing heart, spine, brains and guts. Empty suits.

And politicians, whether they slither back into non-candidacy or march into office, typically forget about the volunteer staff who helped get them there, the kids who are tomorrow's candidates, the wannabes who could be next campaign's competition.

I never felt settled there, was never more confused and alienated. Home to brutal winters – when the bitter winds snapped and whipped at my face, hissing angrily past my ears – and humid poolless summers – when the air felt so sticky it was like pushing through jelly – the nation's capital had little in common with Arizona. Except for termites.

The flicker of politics had pulled me to the east coast, but to survive I turned to what I knew best: bugs. Wood chompers. By then, after years in the business, I was a specialist in wood-destroying organisms, having taken night classes and earned my Mr Termite degree.

Every day I'd slip into my forest-green monkey suit, strap on a twenty-pound tank of bug poison and head out, flashlight in hand, searching for those cellulose-lovers. I rooted around under houses, I crawled through attics, slopped and flopped under crawl-spaces, searching for any and all evidence of my employers, the insects that were simultaneously my best friends and the enemies I was forced to wipe out.

I knew bugs better than I'd once known my own nose. I spent hours sharing with horrified homeowners the insect facts I'd collected. 'The queen termite,' I'd say about a hundred times a week, 'she's as big as a pickle, squirming five feet underground, squeezing out a new termite egg every twenty seconds. For five years. That's over a million termites right under this house. Unless she is stopped.'

Queenie's colony is divided into soldiers, who guard the termite palace, and workers, who head out to gnaw wood, returning every twenty-four hours to hurl the digested housepart at Her Royal Termite's feet. The key, I told the by-then bug-eyed homeowners, was to kill off her reproductive enablers, the workers, and shut down the termite-making machine. The way

I painted her, the queen sounded more horrifying than the Loch Ness monster; and she was, being right there, squeezing out more monsters only a few feet under ours.

Washington, with its old, rotting terraced houses, had termites all right: I saw homes that were riddled with the critters. Houses where every window frame, every doorframe and every beam was hollow.

One time, while I was poking around in an attic, a beam caved in and I fell right through the ceiling and into a frying pan sizzling on the stove. 'Yup, you've got a serious termite problem there, ma'am,' I said to the shocked, spatula-holding missus, whose fried eggs I was now sitting upon. 'And in the time it took me to fall here, that queen just laid three more.' The missus signed up for the full pest-control package.

Being a bugman wasn't my dream job, but I didn't mind it. Until, that is, the juice started making me sick. I was coated with the stuff; three showers couldn't wash off the smell of poison and the stickiness that clung to my skin like a baby termite hanging on to a soldier in a fumicide fog. I had an ongoing insecticide headache, my stomach was coiled, my appetite shrivelled. Every day I'd read about a new toxic horror, realizing that my job environment resembled Love Canal. My co-worker worried out loud that if he had a daughter she'd be born with six tits on her back. At least she'd be popular for slow dances.

I felt like a walking pest strip, and was apparently perceived that way. Mosquitoes didn't bite me, fleas quickly hopped away, roaches stampeded next door. And my girlfriend started to bug off as well.

Sickened by my job, quite literally, I'd take a few months off, then strap on my tank again, only to quit once more, made

nauseous by the fumes I was spraying. Even now that insecticide smell gets to me. Eating bugs doesn't make me gag, but one whiff of that juice makes me hurl.

When I wasn't El Exterminador (the name given me in Spanish-speaking neighbourhoods), I was Mr Let's-Give-This-Baby-a-Spin. A car salesman. Instead of poison I came home reeking of that new-car smell, from continual test drives during those unbearable summer months, when you'd get in and stick to the vinyl, leaving patches of flesh behind when you got out.

And, though I could make more money in cars than in insects, I despised the job. It was horrible. I hated the meetings where managers would pump up the sales staff, saying, 'Shoppers are like grapes. They're to be stepped on and squashed.' I hated the generic reference to 'Mr and Mrs Shithead', and the way a salesjerk would say, 'Oh boy, here comes another mooch.' Car salesmen, trained to view buyers as victims, trained to be automaton selling-machines, are simply cold: a bad credit report would come back with the manager's note scrawled over it: *This is dreck, get them off the lot!* A browser couldn't buy a deflated tire from the sales-sleaze after that.

And I hated the weekly incentives, the fifty-dollar bonuses – called spiffs – handed out whenever a salesman could demonstrate to management his persuasive powers and ability to control customers by persuading shoppers to do something dumb. Like climb into the trunk. Salesmen would do everything except shove a shopper in the trunk, just to get that spiff.

'Look how much room this trunk has,' they'd say in that overwhelming car-sales way, designed to break down defences. 'Think how many suitcases and bags of groceries you can fit in! Imagine how many boxes you could carry back here the

next time you move! Why, you could sneak the kids into drive-in movies if you stashed them back here! Go on – check out the extra room for spare tyres! There's so much room in here, you could camp in it, you could grill in it, you could pitch a tent! Just get on in that trunk and take a close look.' By then they'd be leaning over the trunk and, with a little luck and a slight push, the customer would climb in.

And once the shopper had crawled into the trunk, a voice would boom over the car-lot speaker, 'Paging Dick Smith, paging Dick Smith' – and that was the signal that the manager had caught the stunt, and another $50 would be winging the sales-sleaze's way.

I refused to sell cars their way: not only did I avoid the car-salesman fashion, the white belt, white shoes and pinkie ring, I shunned the hard sell. I didn't push shoppers into trunks, I didn't cram brains with too much information and jam cerebral circuitry, I didn't wear them down or shove them into the driver's seats of cars they didn't want.

I just watched and listened. And when I heard a certain tone, and saw that certain loving look when they gazed at a car, that's when I'd sell my ass off. It worked. They were under the spell of my subtle ether. When I was into it, when I could forget what I was doing, I could sell four cars a day.

The problem was, I felt guilty. Some people have buyer's remorse; I had seller's remorse. Winning at the car-sales game was depressing – unless I'd gotten them a good deal; but a new car that's a good deal is an oxymoron. Every time a buyer drove off the lot, my stomach would twist tighter; I'd wake up in the middle of the night knowing I'd ruined their next five years, selling them wheels they couldn't afford.

One day, looking over at yet another shopper's legs

kicking out of a trunk, I heard that 'Paging Dick Smith' for the last time. I quit, and went back to the bugs.

It was not a happy time. Whether I was Car Seller or the Bugman, I was massively, hideously bummed. I didn't know where I was going – on the highway of life I was a hitchhiker, bearing a sign: WILL GO ANYWHERE. ANYWHERE THAT HAS BUGS. OR CARS. Nothing was clicking. I was stuck. It was 1985, I was twenty-eight and having a hard time growing up.

Politics bored me: I was sick of the slickness, the lies and the feeling of chronically being used for Capitol gain. My jobs were scarcely fulfilling. I spent hours holed up in my terraced house, compensating for my lack of education by delving into the complete works of Solzhenitsyn, Chekhov, Nabokov, Kerouac, Ginsberg and Céline, whose bitter stories seemed like sitcoms compared to mine. I felt like Ivan Denisovich, slogging along, slogging along, waiting for my situation to get better. Life seemed to be taunting me; I knew there was something I was supposed to do, some ambition I was meant to chase after – but my nose, which I'd once known so well, had lost the scent.

The only times I was mildly happy was at parties – telling embarrassing stories about congressmen's houses I'd fumigated that day. DC parties being among the most staid and dull known to man, my stabs at humour were a hit.

But once I returned home I was overwhelmed by that feeling of gloom. Noticing that more and more I was resembling a downward-spiralling Dostoyevskian character, my girlfriend dragged me to Jamaica, where she promptly fell ill and spent the two weeks knocked out in bed.

Left to myself, I'd sometimes wander out of the hotel compound, being swarmed by the local drug pushers, who

murmured, 'I god de bess 'ash, mon, I god de bess.' Some begged, others hawked wood statues or rings, some offered their services to escort you through the grabbing crowds who constantly harassed tourists, making it a risk to leave the hotel compound. Noticing that the locals backed off from some people, I studied their trick and soon pretended to be German, walking the streets, continually uttering, '*Nein, nein*', hassle-free.

Back at the hotel, while my girlfriend sweated off her fever, I spent hours reading Céline in a hammock, being the only apparently uncoupled person around, with no one to talk to except the groundskeepers, who hung around in the shade of the trees, playing rummy for hours. Sheer boredom drove me to showing them the card tricks I hadn't tried since grade school. The next day there were more groundsmen, who'd brought along the maids, waiting for me under the tree wide-eyed and bedazzled by more sleight of hand. By the end of the week I was putting on hour-long card shows under the tree, and they'd tie me up and watch bug-eyed at my escapes; if I'd been there fifty years before, I would have been made king of that island. Or at least head witchdoctor.

That small taste of performing made me more depressed upon returning to DC. Because I longed to do it again. And magic tricks are not the key to the stage. In North America they're the sign of a loser.

My girlfriend read the sign and dumped me. It was the lowest point of my adulthood. At that point I quit caring, and had nothing to lose. Except for the last of my dignity – onstage.

I was wallowing in a black ooze of depression by the time I slunk past the hipsters and beat-punks in a small art bar called D.C. Space. It was the only hip place in town, the only place that had spoken-word open mikes.

The stage was tiny, the lights were dim and, not having performed for years, I was mortified. Worse, I was bad. Real bad. Not confident enough to ad lib, I'd read my pieces from loose notebook paper shaking in my hands. My performances came off as wooden as the cellulose a worker termite hurls. What I lacked in style I made up for in volume.

Most of my ramblings were in the angry-young-man-spews-bad-vibes-loudly genre, and they weren't very credible, since by then I was no longer a particularly young man. I'd read on and on about survival in the urban jungle, my breathy performance punctuated by an occasional redeeming moment, when every so often the audience members would shut up and listen. At least some of them. Sometimes.

The biggest crowd-pleaser in my repertoire was the part about 'bumbience' – the ambience of the bum lifestyle, during which I read poems about a homeless two-car family.

'SHE'S GOT A CAR, HE'S GOT A CAR,' I bellowed from the stage, looking out at the bereted Kerouac-wannabes looking back at the same. 'THEY KISS EACH OTHER SOFTLY AND TURN OUT THE DOME LIGHT.' Sometimes I'd get a laugh out of that one; some nights, two.

But even though my performances generally sucked, I loved being back on the stage. I had few fans, the applause was meagre and the nights my friends didn't show the applause was non-existent. Yet this was the only joy in my life. Every two weeks, when there was another open-mike night, I'd return – slink back onstage and perform my spoken word for an audience who really only wanted to hear Ginsberg's 'Howl'.

It was there on a Wednesday open mike that I met Bebe. Love of my life. The future Circus Queen. Fresh off the plane from France.

I was crazy about her from the second she came into view. She had this look of adventure in her eyes, a gorgeous face, wispy body and a really great butt. And after I approached her, when she opened her mouth, French came out. The way she said my name, 'Zsheem,' made me feel woozier than walking out of a fumigation tent, but in a much better way.

Happily, she seemed to like me. At first. Until I stepped on the stage. The newcomer knew little of my language, but she knew enough to know I was bombing. By the end of the piece, when I walked off, she was gone. But my little Bebe was back the next open mike, and that time I had new ammunition. An act I knew would jolt.

Back then I was living in Du Pont Circle. It was a hodge-podge of somewhat safe blocks next to deadly ones. One block would be home to yuppies busy renovating their homes, the next block you could score the most potent heroin in the city, the next street would be lined with middle-class families, and one street over it was Hooker Heaven.

Pedestrians scurried to their destinations in checkerboard style, skirting the danger blocks. One Saturday as I was hop-scotching along, I detoured and cut through Du Pont Park. It was a glorious spring day, the cherry blossoms in bloom, the birds twittering, the children laughing. I felt like shit.

A crowd had formed around a bench and, nearing it, I saw a young guy waving torches of fire around and shoving the flaming end in his mouth. A fire eater. I hadn't seen one since the Arizona State Fair. And, just like back then, it gave me a jolt.

I went back the next day and hung around watching him for hours, later offering to buy him a beer. Wasn't long before

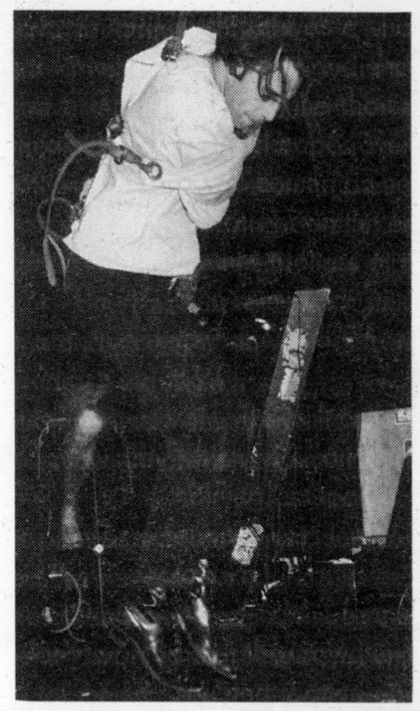

Jim Rose in a straightjacket.
Photo by David Harradine

Sammy J. and I were on first-name terms; he didn't know my last name either. Wasn't long before he revealed to me the secrets of his trade over a pitcher – and the next day actually taught me to extinguish flames with my mouth.

The next Wednesday, when I returned to the stage with blistered lips and sizzled tongue, I was more than just a poet; I was a neophyte fire eater.

'SHE HAD A CAR, HE HAD A CAR,' I bellowed, igniting a cloth baton that made a large *whoosh*. 'THEY KISSED EACH OTHER SOFTLY AND TURNED OUT THE DOME LIGHT.' Then I shoved the ball of fire into my mouth.

It worked. Sort of. Instead of two people clapping, half the crowd was. These people had been born in the 60s; they'd never seen a sideshow. They'd missed out on the Arizona State Fair, they'd never seen anything more spectacular than the pabulum and the pageantry of the traditional American circus. They hadn't even experienced the Beat Generation first-hand.

I could sense the potential of my act, and knew that

Lifto wearing iron earrings.
Photo by David Harradine

somehow I'd almost struck a cord that even the best 'Howl'-ers weren't striking. And that night, after my show, Bebe agreed to go out. As long as I didn't try to kiss her until my mouth burns healed.

Thanks to aloe vera we moved in together that month, and were married the next year by a drunk judge who put the wrong date on the certificate, but we regarded it as official none the less.

Being from France, Bebe opened a door that I hadn't known existed. She turned me on to the street performers, the European-style circus and fakirs.

They were everywhere in Europe, she told me, you couldn't go to the corner fruit stand without bumping into somebody doing something amazing. There were people there actually doing the stunts I'd only seen in worn photos. My scrapbook had grown much bigger by then due to Bob Blackmar, an old carny who'd given me copies of his collection. I wanted to see this stuff in person.

Her stories were intriguing. I felt the lure. I put down my juice tank, drove back to the car lot, went on a selling streak and saved up enough money for a two-month trip overseas.

France saved my ass. It gave me a sense of mission, and slapped ambition and a love of life back into me. It's hard to be depressed in that country, unless your name is Céline or Sartre. And, unlike DC, France was more awesome than a postcard. The smell of cooling bread wafting through the streets, the *bonbons* in windows alongside glazed fruit tarts and sugar-dusted éclairs, the rich *café crème*, the bistros and cafés where the morning paper is discussed through the day, the Gothic steeples shooting into the sky, the balconies that peeked out from medieval buildings, the cobblestoned squares where performers gathered, the sound of church bells always ringing. I was nearly as in love with the country as with the woman who had brought me to it. My lovely Bebe; I'd probably still be Bugboy without her.

She had come from a circus family of sorts: her sister rode the unicycle, her brother-in-law juggled and spun plates on sticks, and they sometimes travelled with a German troupe called Randilini's. And being from a family of ten kids, she lined up places to stay across the continent.

We took a train to the south of France, where the Riviera meets the Mediterranean. There, along the boardwalk, we found mimes, jugglers and accordion players; they were mildly amusing, but not what I'd come to see. But we stayed longer, hoping to see more. One day at the end of the strip I met a fakir; at least that's what he said he was – but he struck me as a faker. The true fakirs are religious holy men from the Middle East; this guy seemed to be a turbaned hoax. Besides,

he wasn't real friendly, and wasn't giving me any clues about how he sprinkled seeds in his palm, closed it and made a daisy of harmony appear. He did, however, tell me where most of the street performers were; since it was off-season at the beach, many had headed to Paris.

We hopped a north-bound overnight train, and it was there – in Paris – that I found the street scene I'd been searching for.

Paris is the Manhattan of Europe – a magnet for the colourful and bizarre. And you could find the strangest of street performers in mass quantities at Beaubourg, the sprawling square shooting off behind the Pompidou Centre. There, not far from fountains that squirt water from pairs of lips, I met performers who came from the Middle East, from Fiji, from Australia and Africa, to perform in Paris, giving me a snapshot of the strange stunts of the world. There was one guy from Africa who'd let a spectator hold open his eyes while someone else dumped in buckets of dirt. He'd twitch for a second, then tears streamed down his face. The next second he'd blink and be fine. His secret was microwaving the dirt and wearing clear contacts. And his stage, a pile of dirt, got higher every time he performed. By the end of the day his stage was four feet high and he looked like a survivor of the Oklahoma dust bowl; if you patted him on the back you'd send smoke signals. He was the opposite of an 'easy mark' – if you patted his back, *he* left a mark on *your* hand.

And a bit beyond him a stocky Frenchman with a waxed curlicue moustache was eating light bulbs. A crowd had formed around the performer, a husky guy in his forties with a blubbery stomach that he could wriggle around or make stick out so far he looked like a pregnant woman three months

Bebe and Jim Rose eating fire.
Photo by Alison Braun

overdue. He pulled handfuls of worms out of his pocket and ate them; he fake-sneezed and waved around arms dripping with fake bogeys. He was a gross-out artist extraordinaire.

I didn't care about the stomach stuff, the worm stuff or the bogeys. I wanted to know how to eat glass.

I gave him a big tip. And we returned the next day, and the day after that. His name was Bruno, and by the third day he recognized us and our hefty tips. We quickly befriended him, but he wouldn't pass on his knowledge for free. We struck a deal: if we helped him pass the hat after his shows, he'd teach me how to eat light bulbs.

Bebe and I spent hours every day watching Bruno's geek act while tourists waddled along in that way tourists do, saying that same tourist stuff they always say: 'Oh, honey, look, it's the Arch d'Triumph! Oh, honey, look, it's the Louvre! Oh, honey, look, it's a guy eating worms! Let's watch.'

I hid my true feelings about most of Bruno's act, but when it came to that chomping-on-glass part I put down his hat and picked up my notebook. I could have written a book on the art of eating light bulbs by the end of a week – how he first broke them in a bag, and slowly chewed the shards like a cow, milking the crunch-filled mastication for maximum effect as if in an ad for potato chips.

Since Bruno spoke only French, part of my job was to translate his stunts to the English speakers in the crowds. 'Bruno the Fearless Frenchman!' I bellowed. 'His ancestors performed these same dangerous stunts for the crowns of Europe centuries ago – chomping light bulbs for Louis XIV and Henry the VIII.' Nobody ever pointed out the impossibility of eating light bulbs in an era when the world was candle-lit. Sometimes I'd throw in non sequiturs from the old days. 'Big

Chainsaw football.
Photo by David Harradine

Bruno, he's big, he's fat, he's happy – ha ha ha. Takes six men to hug him and a boxcar to lug him! Found in the Grand Canyon of Tucson, Arizona – Big Bruno!'

My translation duties also included explaining the meaning of a passed hat; English speakers like to pretend it's a foreign concept that they don't quite grasp.

Between Bebe's good looks and my ability to harass the English speakers we doubled his income, which sometimes came to $200 a day.

Bruno was elated and rewarded us by buying bottles of Sancerre in a nearby café where candles beamed from wine bottles and where, as in most every European café, there were two sets of prices, tourist and local; he passed on his discount. There, over glasses of the wine that smelled vaguely like cat

piss, sitting around wooden tables with century-old graffiti carved in them, night by night he taught me the art of how to eat glass without shredding my tongue.

Since he spoke only French, I relied on Bebe for translations – and when you're learning how to eat glass, you realize how much you trust your translator and her fluency. My last week there, I went through a bag of light bulbs at that café, while Bruno guided my every chomp.

Later, as the skies turned inky black, his friends would stumble in – a sword swallower, a fakir, an Albanian contortionist. European street performers hang together, usually haunting the same bistros. Even the mimes and jugglers were tolerable after sunset, and they sat down for a swig as well.

Before, I'd just wanted to learn how these stunts worked; now I'd decided to write a book about the strange. Through Bebe I interviewed them all with the zeal of a cub reporter, hastily jotting down their history and the secrets handed down from generation to generation. Some had spent years altering their bodies – like the sword swallower who had manipulated his gag reflex. Some had learned ancient knowledge, which, under the guise of religion, they refused to reveal. Some were illusionists, some were true human marvels; others were straight-up con artists.

Sitting around that café, I even learned some of the secrets of gypsies. One night the door swung open and a hippie girl breezed through, crying and asking about a Mademoiselle Rosette she had met there the week before. In her hands she twisted a bandanna as she lamented that something had gone wrong with Rosette's spell.

Bruno, who himself looked to be part gypsy, laughed at the sight. 'The poor fool – she's been taken by the oldest gypsy

scam,' he said via Bebe. The gypsies, he said, always explain that whatever your problem is it can be solved by money. And they tell you they have a secret method to double, triple, maybe even quadruple it. You hand them a hundred in bills, and they wrap it in a bandanna for you, stitching it together with incantation and magic powders and wrapping a strand of hair around it. And they tell you to sleep with it under your pillow for a week to change your fortune. A week later, when you rip open the bandanna, expecting the money to have multiplied, you find that it was switched at the original meeting and this bandanna is a different one stuffed with paper. By then the gypsy's long gone.

I was intrigued – and added that to my notes. Every day we were in Paris I took copious notes, and hauled out entire shelves of library books which Bebe translated for me at night.

I was obsessed, a man on a jolt trip. I knew that, commonplace though these stunts were in Europe, they would be mind-boggling in North America.

When we returned to DC, I had two suitcases brimming with loose paper covered with my chicken scrawls. And I had a new act: eating glass.

'SHE HAD A CAR, HE HAD A CAR,' I bellowed from the stage of a new club, a tiny speakeasy called Javarama. 'BUT SOMEBODY KNOCKED OUT HER REAR WINDOW.' And then I'd bite into a bulb, cracking into the mike for a nice crispy glass sound, and gulp it down with a pained look. The audience groaned and squirmed in their seats. All of them. I knew I was on to something, that, even though I didn't know exactly where I was going, I was running on the right track.

I studied those notes as thoroughly as an honours student

before finals. The book idea didn't intrigue me so much any more; I wanted to perform. But even though I knew the theory behind the other stunts I wanted to learn, I wasn't foolish enough to try them alone, without the supervision of a master. I needed more people to teach me, many more Brunos.

So I went back to the car lot, went on another selling streak and saved up enough money to return to Europe. This time for three months. And this time I didn't want just to observe the street scene; limited though my repertoire was, I wanted to be part of it.

In Barcelona there's a bustling cobblestone strip called Las Ramblas that is screaming with colour and non-stop entertainment. Bars and cafés, where the locals sit drinking early-morning port and smoking cigarettes, line the tree-lined promenade, parakeet cages are parked outside every shop, bouquets of flowers burst from buckets, the farmers pile up tomatoes, peppers and bunches of cilantro, the seafood is heaped high on ice, and the local hustlers set up boxes for three-card *monte*. Loaded with tourists and sunny most of the year, it's a haven for street performers.

Our first days there, we arrived every morning and sat at a sidewalk café, drinking *cafe con leche*, waiting for the street life to unfold and trying to befriend the locals. Initially I was eyed suspiciously, but I quickly built up street-level trust, by never exposing the three-card-*monte* guys, who dealt cards on cardboard boxes and would often shill hundreds from tourists trying to guess which of the three cards before them was the queen of hearts. The minute they scored big, one of the *monte* mob would yell '¡Policía!' and they'd scramble down an alley, leaving their boxes and the open-mouthed mark behind. There were mimes and guys with shell scams, luring

tourists with pick-the-one-with-the-pea patter.

There was a big burly guy with tufts of hair growing out of his nose who called himself 'the Human Dartboard' and never winced when he was slammed with darts. There was a short little guy with beady eyes who swallowed razor blades. There were mimes, jugglers and puppeteers. There were con artists everywhere – even a sweet-smiling old-timer running the family shoe store, who would sell you a pair, but when you returned home it was merely a shoebox filled with rocks. Like the gypsy, he'd pulled a switch. But it was non-stop entertainment.

The crudest and most colourful of them all was the Fat Lady. As big as Big Bertha and toothless as well, her face was pasty and scarred, and her matted hair, the few strands that were left, had the colour and smell of piss. Her outfit was always the same: she wore underwear only, underwear with the elastic stretched out, underwear that was ripped and grey. She was invariably drunk, regardless of the hour; and she knew how to stay that way. As tourists paraded by, perusing the wallet stands or gypsy palm readers, she would find a handsome man in the bunch, and cling to him like spat-out bubble gum. She'd throw her arm around him and belch in his face. She'd grab at his hand and kiss it. She'd whip up her bra and flash a sagging tit. She'd follow him on hands and knees until he ran down the street.

She was Las Ramblas's court jester. But she wasn't stupid. After she'd chased her victim away, she returned to all the sidewalk bistros and cafés, where onlookers were wild with laughter, and passed her hat. It was always brimming by the time she got it back.

And it hit me how different the street scene was in

Europe. In the US, nobody would have laughed, nobody would have applauded, nobody would have given her the time, much less a dime. They would have felt sorry, they'd have tried to ignore her, the dutiful might have called the police. But in Barcelona she filled the niche of the village idiot – though she was sharp enough to milk it and make a living.

By the third day of studying the scene I was ready to join in. Bebe wrapped me up in a straitjacket – and I writhed and wriggled to get out, while a few bystanders watched. I chomped light bulbs, while more gathered around. I ate fire – and finally pulled out what I considered my lamest act: card tricks. And then I passed my hat and scored enough pesetas for dinner.

By sunset, when we settled in for paella and late-night port, while classical guitarists strummed from alleyways, the street performers were coming up to me. They didn't want to know about light bulbs or fire-eating. They wanted to know about card tricks. So I traded my secrets for theirs, once again jotting down notes. There in one week I learned not only how to add chains to my escape act, but also gained the nerve to try the Human Dartboard.

We returned to the boardwalk in France, where I performed with Bebe's sister and brother, who revealed the secrets of unicycling (practice) and plate-spinning (practice again). This time it was summer; the place was swimming with fakirs. After days of me filling his turban, one finally told me the secret of lying on a bed of nails, and how to construct one. We stayed there a few days, lounging about while he taught me the art.

The next week we travelled to Freiburg in Germany, where we sat around taking in the sights of the main square.

The scene was the same except that, instead of classical guitar the music was Bavarian, instead of paella we ate bratwurst, and instead of sipping port we chugged lager. And there were no parakeets or Fat Ladies there. One night, while drinking stout in the local beer hall, I met a so-called human blockhead, who swapped knowledge of how to pound nails up his nose for learning how to eat glass.

Later that week we hopped a train for Amsterdam, and there in the red-light district I found an American who not only ate glass but threw his face in it and let people stand on the back of his head. He was a tough negotiator: I had to trade the secret of the blockhead, and the bed of nails, for him to tell me how to do the face-in-glass without shredding my mug beyond recognition.

I'd filled five notebooks by the time Bebe and I showed up at her parents' in a suburb of Angers, where I quickly built a gnarly bed of nails and went through the rigours of skin-toughening for face-in-glass. Most in-laws would have thought their daughter had married a nut, but I was a huge hit at the next week's family reunion.

Back in DC, when I next took the stage at Javarama and unveiled my bag of tricks, the crowd went berserk. By then I'd permanently parked my car poems, and was trying out the patter I'd learned on Europe's sidewalks.

My opener was 'You look like a jaded fuck – verify this is a real hammer and a real nail.' And then I unleashed a fast-paced whirlwind show. They were jolted. Entirely amped. Well, that's how it seemed to me; in fact, I did have a small following. But I was sick of DC. Javarama was the only place to perform – and they had open mike once a month. I wanted more venues and more practice. It was early summer, the heat

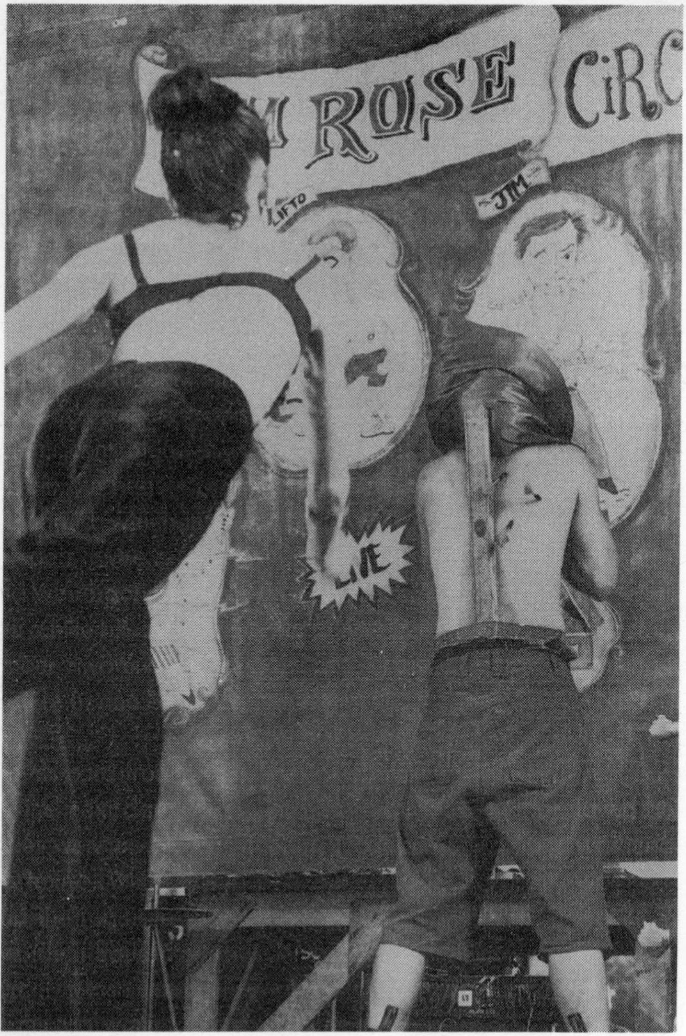

Jim Rose doing human dartboard with Bebe Rose throwing darts.
Photo by Jeffoto

was already oppressive, the city already overwhelmed by sickening street smells. And the crime was hitting all-time highs. One day there were six drive-by shootings, and I'd walked past four of the sites earlier that day.

After seven years in DC I was ready to leave. And head to a land where the street performers were bathed in gold. Venice. Venice Beach, California. Where I could perform six shows a day.

Jim Rose as human Blockhead.
Photo by Bebe Rose

CHICKEN LEGS AND TOWELS FOR RENT

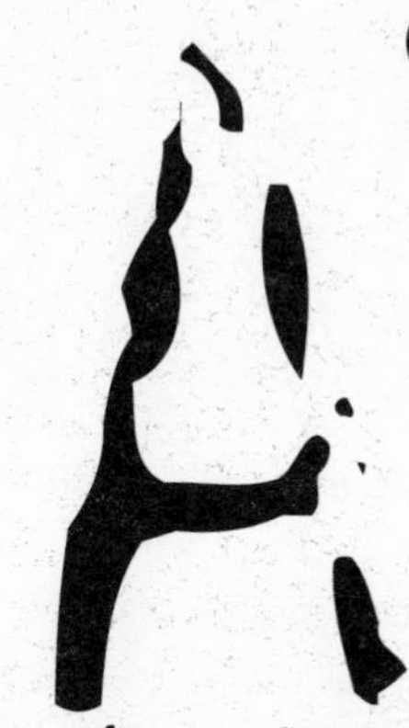

h, Venice Beach. June 1990. The ocean crashed into the surf, the palm trees swayed in the summer breeze and the throngs of tourists flooded the boardwalk. It was heaven. Until I heard a godawful noise.

A noise that was a cross between Chinese folk singer and a yodeller, a voice more shrill than Tiny Tim's. The screeching was coming from the wide-open mouth of a tall Rollerblader, clad in a white robe, with penetrating blue eyes peeking out from the turban wrapped around his head. The annoyer-on-wheels whipped in and out of the parade of strolling tourists, electric guitar in hand, speaker dangling from his belt, circling a couple, his designated prey. He hovered, humiliating them with his semi-musical shrieks, and was unrelenting in his high-decibel serenade until he'd embarrassed them out of a five spot. And then he skated off – to ruin another lovey-dovey couple's special moment.

Venice Beach was a zoo, a madhouse, a mile-long strip of the showiest, most egotistical performers in the country wedged side by side, performers competing for attention and money, all trying to outdo each other. That cement ribbon of Pacific-hugging boardwalk west of LA was a pulsating snake of eccentricity: palm readers, hair wrappers, sand sculptors, break-dancers, baton twirlers, jugglers, flexing musclemen, flipping gymnasts, mimes, comedians, accordions, skateboarder daredevils, unicyclists, and trillions of Rollerbladers, of which Hari Kari, the shrieking serenader, was by far the most obnoxious.

Tourists by the thousands poured on to the strip, tossing dollars and change into the hats laid down before them. 'Chicken legs' – that's what the locals called them because of their sickly pale skin. So many cruised down this strip that Venice Beach was the second-largest tourist attraction in California, behind only Disneyland. It was a street performer's paradise.

I was finally there to do the big show. The show I'd been working on for a year. Here on Venice Beach I could put on as many shows as I wanted, as many as the crowds demanded. I figured they'd be begging for ten, twenty, a day.

At first I was a little worried. Since the beach was a free-enterprise zone, one of the few foot-traffic centres in the nation that tolerated street performers, I would be competing against the top-notch buskers from across the land.

But strolling along the beach, taking in the chainsaw juggler, the fire eater who could balance a bicycle on his chin, the bug eater and even the limbo king who jumped around in glass, I felt smug.

Because the one and only thing Venice Beach didn't

have was my act. And it was the real thing – authentic feats learned in the streets of Europe from the masters, acts that were gonna blow the masses away. Nobody else was doing anything like I was. For my first show I would put my face in glass, pound a screwdriver up my nose, lie on a bed of nails and have people stand on top of me. Those stunts alone were more than any other show on that beach could offer, more entertainment than you could find anywhere. I figured that would turn me into a rage. All I had to do was stick my basket out there, and retrieve it at the end of the day. I was gonna clean up. These thoughts looped around and around in my head like a salesman's self-promotional tape.

With $600 to our names Bebe and I checked into a cheesy motel two blocks from the beach. Our room was tiny, the size of a closet, so small the cockroaches were hunchbacked. The only piece of furniture was the lumpy bed with springs bursting out; tacky seascapes adorned the walls, which were so thin you could hear the neighbours screwing and beating each other up all night. It was heaven. Or so it seemed, because I was on a manic high – having finally landed where I knew I should be. I was going to rock. I was going to rule. Starting *mañana*, I'd be the most sizzling act on the beach for the whole summer.

I had a few things to learn. And the first thing I learned on Venice Beach is that you need to get into a fistfight every morning just to get your spot.

After taking in the scene that first day, I'd thought I'd figured it out. There were no booths to rent, no lottery to pick your space. It was survival of the slickest, and the quickest. Whoever gets there earliest gets the spot. So I ran to the boardwalk at six the next morning – and, except for the sea –

gulls swooping, the old men with metal detectors sweeping and the joggers sweating, the place was deserted.

But everywhere along the boardwalk there were towels. I figured they'd washed up during high tide, though I wondered how so many people could lose their towels in one day. Then I noticed they each had tape on them. And on each strip of tape was a name.

It dawned on me that these spots were theoretically reserved – with towels marking the claims. Vacant towels without humans to guard them.

This would never have gone over in DC, in New York, in Europe or anywhere else. A dinky, ragged little towel – even with a name taped on it – does not a reservation make. So I ignored them – and promptly set up my bed of nails at a prime location near the Asian food stands. An hour later the contortionist whose towel I'd kicked aside showed up and booted me off his space. I moved on without hassle. There were other towels to claim. I set up again, not far away, but at nine the juggler whose towel had been down showed up and likewise bade me *sayonara*. I moved on down the strip and the same thing happened over and over, with everybody snarling at me, 'Hey, man, that's my space!' and holding up their towel as if it were a real-estate title.

Finally there was only one towel left that no human was sitting on. I stomped to that towel, claimed it as my space and set up. This spot I was ready to fight for, because there was nowhere else to go.

Well, they were big, they were mean, they were break-dancers. And when they showed up an hour later, they kinda wanted that towel-reserved space of theirs back. I explained that they couldn't reserve a spot with a towel; I argued that I'd been there first, so that spot was mine. I pleaded to let me have it 'cause that was the right thing to do. I tried to amuse them, showing them how I could pound a nail up my nose.

The trio of young toughs remained unconvinced and unmoved, noting that it would be even easier for me to pound stuff up my nose after they'd shot a bullet through it. So they got their spot back.

I packed up my bed of nails, my hammer, my bag of bulbs, shuffled back to the motel and then headed out again to figure out how this deal worked. That whole day I just cruised back and forth across the beach, watching shows and trying to chat with my neighbours.

Unlike the Europeans, these street performers were initially very territorial and not a helpful bunch; they were like alley cats, each one pissing an invisible line, and ready to take out anyone who challenged it. And I was like a little puppy dog wagging its tail, wanting to join in their scene. Finally a chainsaw juggler, sick of the panting puppy, tipped me off. He told me about Mom.

That's what everyone called her, the sweet, plump, hunchbacked old woman who lived down the way in a shack. She was the one who put out the towels every night at 3 a.m. And though she looked unthreatening – dressed in a ratty pink robe, her hair in curlers, her slippers always sliding one step in front of her foot – her word packed a wallop. Mom ruled the boardwalk, being the unofficial landlord of the beach, dispensing justice left and right. And she had plenty of locals who supported her power – locals who'd grown up with Mom, borrowed money from Mom, and locals who wanted to keep the status quo towel-as-reservation system in effect, so they could just slide in and set up on their towel at noon.

I traipsed over to Mom's beach bungalow to apply for a space. Unfortunately, it being the high tourist season, everything was rented. Fortunately, some guy – a watercolourist, I believe – was behind on his rent. I tossed her $10 for the day, and she ripped off the piece of tape with his name on it and stuck on a piece with mine. And she tossed down the ripped blue towel with my name taped on it the next morning.

So I got my spot. I finally got my spot. A good spot too – midway along the strip, right by Westminster Street, just down the way from Gold's Gym, where the musclemen flexed their glistening pecs in the sun for all the beach babes to see.

Bebe and I went out that night and celebrated with a pricy meal beachside – living it up with steak and lobster and bottles of wine, because I'd finally made it to Venice Beach, and knew the next day my coffers would be brimming with traveller's cheques and tourist dollars. The next morning I laid down a red tarp and set up my bed of nails, arranged my bag of light bulbs and nose-pounding equipment, and then – without announcement or much ado – I began, knowing that the chicken legs would swarm around when they caught sight of what I could do.

First I pounded a screwdriver up my nose, then I threw my face in a pile of glass and had Bebe stand on my head. Then I lay on the bed of nails, and for the grand finale I made an escape from a straitjacket that was chained. When I began, nobody was watching; when I ended, nobody was watching. My wicker basket that I'd put out for donations remained empty.

Undaunted, I started again: pounding the screwdriver up my nose, throwing my face in glass, lying on the bed of nails, writhing to escape a straitjacket. Once again, nobody was there at beginning or end. I performed my act again – more indignantly this time – and still nobody was watching. Thousands of people strolled right by me, and with little more than a nervous glance they all kept on strolling. But my basket wasn't empty: a seagull flew by and crapped in it.

'Don't worry, Jim,' Bebe consoled me. 'Tomorrow will be a better day. In France bird shit is good luck.' I love the French; they could find a lucky meaning in an air-raid siren.

So I came back the next morning, hoping that the bird-shit luck would kick in. I set up and started my show but, once again, nobody cared. They kept walking by, waddling by, running by, skating by. When Bebe stood on my head while my face was in glass, a couple sidled up hand-in-hand and sneered that if they wanted that kind of entertainment they'd go to an insane asylum. By the end of the day my basket was emptier than before; even the seagulls were snubbing me. 'Maybe luck only comes from the shit of French birds,' I joked.

Bebe got that red-nosed look that alerts that she's about to cry, and frankly I felt the same way. 'What are we going to do?' she asked.

'Aw, Bebe, don't worry,' I lied, 'tomorrow will be better.' We slunk back to the motel, not saying a word. That night our neighbours were banging into the wall with such force that our lumpy bed was shaking with theirs as if we were having a wall orgy. I couldn't sleep and stayed up all night figuring out what was wrong.

I didn't know at the time that performing on the street in the US is a lot different from performing onstage. Ground-level acts have to snag the audience, and then lure their trust. And whenever people would wander by my spot, and see the tools of my trade – the bed of nails and the jagged mountain of

glass – they'd pick up their pace. If their interest was even slightly piqued, they'd watch me from fifty yards away – as if I'd be tossing their ass in the glass.

So I was having a horrible time getting a crowd. My shows became only practice; even Bebe was bored being my sole fan as I ran through my routine over and over, waiting vainly for an audience to gather. By the afternoon Bebe looked dejected, fingering designs in the sand. I noticed they were arrows, all pointing down. She refused to stand on my head. 'What's the point?' she asked. 'Nobody's looking.'

That night as I lay on the lumpy bed watching the spiders weave in the corner, I figured out a fundamental rule of performing: being able to market what you do is more important than what you actually do. It took me about six hours of lost sleep – while the Italian couple one thin wall away wailed, 'DIO MIO, DIO MIO!' into the night – to figure that out.

Next day I was back, shaking with piss and vinegar, loudly yelling, 'The wonders of Europe are here before you! I'm Jimmy the Geek, here to show you the secrets passed down from generation to generation!' Well, that got a few chicken legs' attention, but once I started pounding stuff up my nose they'd bolt.

So I regrouped. While Bebe guarded the gear, I cruised back along the beach, studying performer after performer, seeing how they pulled in their crowd.

A half-mile down I heard loud calypso tunes like you'd hear in Trinidad. A crowd was forming around a slight man with a pencil-thin moustache parked on his upper lip. It was Perry Hernandez, the Ambassador of Limbo. As I peered through the throng, I was amazed. He wasn't doing anything. Except sweeping. Perry was sweeping off his area with a broom with such energy, giving you the feeling that something incredible was going to happen any minute. An anticipation crept through the crowd – why is he a sweeping fiend, what is he going to do? All the while the Ambassador of Limbo didn't so much as look up, letting them be sucked into the mystery without explanation.

After five minutes, when 150 or so had gathered around, he tossed down the broom, picked up his limbo stick and started to dance. The audience was snared: they'd spent so much time waiting for the show, they weren't going to leave till it was through.

The Ambassador inadvertently passed on a key to the crowd-building process: don't look. Eye contact intimidates passers-by, they feel too intimate and walk away; so don't look. At least until you have thirty or more gathered around, wondering what the hell you're doing and why you're not looking at them. Take time setting stuff up. Appear very busy and worried, like something huge is going to happen that's potentially very dangerous. That's what I'd been doing wrong: I'd been eyeing the crowd like a hawk, and by the end of my unwatched act it was with that pitiful, pleading look in my eye that inaudibly conveyed, 'Don't go, please don't go, stay.' It was as effective as the sobbing boyfriend clinging to his bolting girlfriend's knee.

So I darted out with some of our precious last dollars, bought a tape player like Perry had, and a tape. And when I went back to my towel, I dragged out the bed of nails and started measuring it, adjusting each nail with a pair of pliers. I measured, adjusted, measured, adjusted, dinked around some more.

And that day I got a crowd – not a big one, mind you, but

at least there was a gradual assembly. As soon as I had twenty or thirty gathered around, I'd say, 'It's showtime, everybody take five steps forward, let's go!' That's another key of crowd control – you have to exert your authority, always make them move around, and leave no question that you are their leader. But at that point I didn't have a well-talked act.

There I was doing the most spectacular things on Venice Beach, but then the crowd would start jeering me, challenging me, heckling me. And they would walk away right when I was asking for the money. I didn't know how to react. It was pathetic. Oh God, it was pathetic. I was almost ready to throw in the watercolourist's towel.

It was, after all, my fifth day on Venice Beach, and I still hadn't done a complete show with people sticking around long enough for me to pass the hat. I was spending \$40 a day on rent, and \$10 to my illegal landlord, not making a cent. I had less than \$100 left, and Bebe and I were surviving on little more than oranges and bananas.

And it was so damn hot, oppressively hot, ridiculously hot – it's Venice Beach, for Christ's sake, and I'm out there doing six shows a day for nothing, working harder than anybody. I tried to be optimistic and remember at least I could get a crowd. Now, if I could only get them to stay, and pay. At night while my neighbours were groaning next door, I paced the room thinking of lines to pull them in and comebacks to shut them up. 'Hey, I don't knock the sailors' cocks out of your mouth when *you're* working!' I'd yell to invisible hecklers. I'd bellow stuff like that through the night. Bebe thought I was nuts.

By the end of the weekend I could talk my way through a show and have enough control to keep spectators throughout. But I still didn't have enough influence to get them to drop much in that cap. My second week there, I was doing almost forty shows a week – and maybe making $50 a day. Just breaking even. It wasn't enough to survive. Bebe and I cut back to two bananas.

Hunger and anger, I found, are the two great motivators. And I was feeling both. My third week on the beach, fuelled by a desire to eat pasta or pizza or beef or anything but bananas, I was getting better with presentation. It was a semi-amusing show at this point. 'I'm Jimmy the Geek,' I'd yell. 'Kids, stay in school – or you'll end up like me.' The kindest of hearts would drop a little money, but not a lot. Most of it was pennies and dimes, maybe the occasional quarter. It sometimes added up to $70 a day. We went back to three bananas – and added oranges and croissants.

Conversion and sidewalk banking became a daily ritual. I joined into the mini-economy on the beach, trading change for bills from the boardwalk merchants, hoping they wouldn't notice my Canadian dimes.

Venice Beach, I was discovering, is the toughest place in the world to make it. Just like on a typical car lot there were only one or two guys making all the money, and the other thirty lived hand-to-mouth. There's no in-between: you're either real good at it, or ought to get another job. I wondered if I had the true desire to be real good at this and scratch out a living.

Week three was a gut-check period. I wasn't getting good enough fast enough. I knew what was holding me back, but it was a difficult line to cross. I noticed that of all the performers only three were good at collecting money. And I studied the techniques they used to get bills out of pockets and into their hats.

Their secret: they turned collection into such a comical

event, it was a show unto itself. They had different ways to entice their audience into paying, and they all had a gimmick. One guy, the chainsaw juggler, had a big plastic bat and he'd hit the cheapos over the head with it if they didn't pay. Another guy, a comedian named Michael Collier, had a long stick with a snatcher on the end – and sections of the crowd would hold up their dollars at the same time, and he'd grab them like a long-armed lobster. 'The green wave', it's called. Another guy, the Mime from Iran, squirt-gunned the ones who didn't pay.

They all collected their dough right before the final stunt, which was pitched as though everything seen before was nothing compared to what was about to happen. That was enough of a lure to keep the chicken legs planted, continuing to take the abuse.

And the formula was so heavy-handed that most people paid; the crowd enjoyed watching the stingy ones be abused, squirted, batted and humiliated with lines like 'Reverend, it's just like church – put the money in the basket,' or 'Oh, look here, everybody – this one's tighter than frog pussy – and that's waterproof.'

It worked. I started making $75, sometimes $100 a day, and could cut back to three shows. Thank God, because I was exhausted.

Those were the days when life on Venice Beach was pretty sweet. Bebe and I would sit on the beach in the morning, drinking *lattes*, eating croissants, listening to Edith Piaf. In the evenings we'd rent bicycles and ride along the beach. I was reading books by the dozen about sideshows and stunts, and was also learning many foreign languages; thanks to our motel neighbours, who came from around the

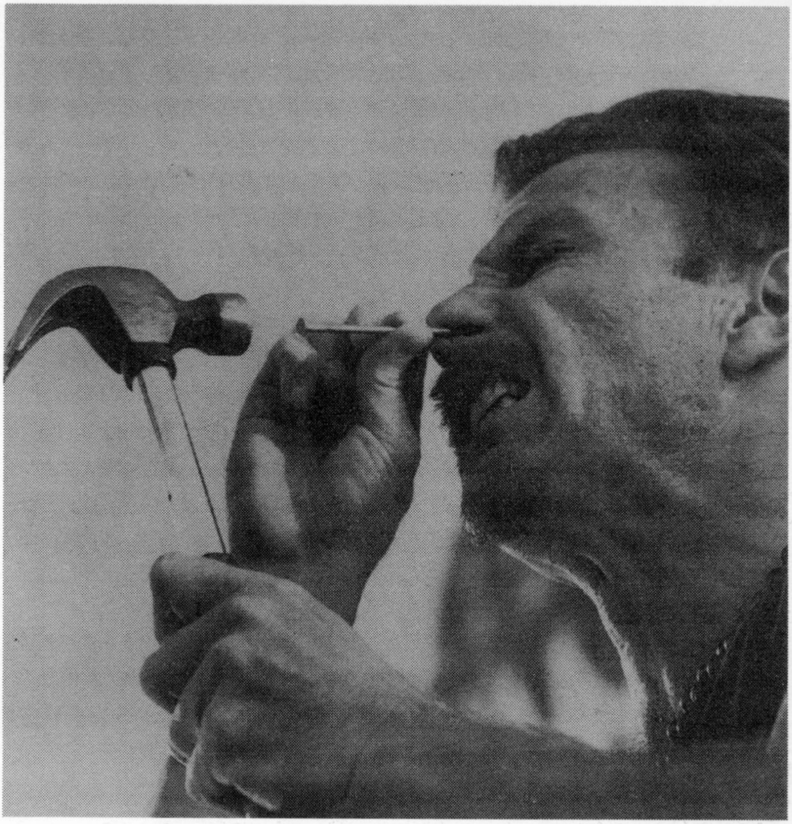

Jim Rose doing human blockhead at Lollapalooza.
Photo by Jeffoto

world, I could say, 'My God!' and 'Fuck me!' in dozens of tongues.

I wanted something more, but I couldn't put my finger on what it was. Life was so laid-back and blissful that I didn't care to figure it out.

One afternoon, a brutally hot one, a roly-poly fellow waddled my way. I'd noticed him at my last show – observing among other things that he didn't donate to my cause and that his attire was that of a car salesman, right down to the pinkie ring. Despite the fact this was California the guy was tanless, and on that fat, swollen white face were a pair of black-rimmed, oversized glasses that magnified his beady eyes.

'Hey, geekie,' he said in a manner reminiscent of a carny. 'I'm an agent. And I'm gonna make you huge. HUUUUUUUUUUUGE!' He extended his chubby hand, which was so pasty it looked like a biscuit with fingers. 'We're gonna take you all over the world, geekie, and we're gonna make you huge. I'm gonna have to work with ya a little bit. But when I'm through, you're gonna be huge. The money won't be great in the beginning, but soon, geekie-boy, you're gonna be huge, huge, huge, huuuuuuuuuge.'

With promises of grandeur he flipped out his card from that pudgy biscuit hand, and said to stop by the next day. There was something seedy about him; my hopes were up.

He lived in Beverly Hills, in a pretty nice house, which wasn't grand or palatial but none the less had the requisite pool, the deck, the carport with a red Jaguar inside. I figured his biz must have been doing OK. But he certainly wasn't at the top of the heap: his house wasn't that big, his Jag wasn't that new and his pool wasn't that clean.

So he sat me down at his sprawling oak desk, lit up a

cigar and then proceeded to take, and make, a few hundred phone calls, telling everybody how he loved them, kiddo, and all the while winking at me.

An hour and a half of teleschmooze later he finally put down the phone. When he turned to me, his tone suddenly changed entirely, and sombreness slid over his face.

'Let's go in the living room and talk,' he said, guiding me into the room where Bebe had been forced to wait all along. He cleared his throat, relit his cigar and exhaled a large plume. 'Listen here, geekie,' he said, 'I gotta tell you the truth. Your act is shit. You're a shitty performer and your presentation is worse. It's gonna take a lot of work to polish this turd, and I don't know if I got the time, or the energy, to make you huge.'

My jaw was scraping the white shag carpet, my ego had slithered under the console. 'Yeah, geekie,' he said, 'I'm not sure what we can do to help you out, but I'll give it some thought. Why don't you give me a call next week. In the mean time, how about I borrow your wife?'

As if he'd hit the instant eject button, Bebe and I bounced up from the couch and headed for the door. It was clear the only thing he'd hoped to make huuuuuuge was his dick inside my wife.

I vowed right there that I'd make myself a name without his.

I kept studying the gimmick guys, and perfecting my crowd-control abilities. By early August I'd figured it out. The last week's totals were more than a grand.

But, you know, I wasn't enjoying it. All the hoopla and persuasion, all the crowd-control techniques – that wasn't why I was an entertainer. It was starting to feel like car sales. The summer was closing, the peak tourist season dying down, and

it would be hard earning much from the locals, who typically paid us in fruit.

I was antsy, once again falling victim to wanderlust. Then I heard of a festival up in Seattle. Something called Bumbershoot.

WELCOME TO FROSTYVILLE

When people think of Seattle, a flurry of images from glossy magazines flutters through their minds.

Seattle, the gorgeous port city shrouded with crystal-blue lakes and carpeted in velvety green. Seattle, the glassy urban gem trapped between two mountain ranges stretching like snow-capped steak knives. Seattle, the land of coffee stands on every street corner, where the hissing of milk is as deafening as the roaring of buses.

In rock mags it's the home of Kurt, bless his soul, and Eddie and Chris – the birthplace of Pearl Jam, Nirvana, Soundgarden and Alice in Chains. It was here that 'grunge' (a word that now makes the residents cringe) first crawled above ground, here that the attractive ripped-jeans-and-never-wash-your-hair look was supposedly born. In travel mags it's praised for the open-air Pike Place Market that spans six city blocks – where apples, wild mushrooms and fresh herbs are piled high,

Dolly the Doll Lady.
Photo by Mark Van-S, Seattle WA

and the scents of gourmet coffee, oranges and baking bread mingle with the smells of tour groups, passed-out transients and sockeye salmon decked out on ice. Its trademarks are the slimy slug and the Jetson-like syringe called the Space Needle.

But the real selling point for us was that in Seattle we had a place to live for free.

Back in the DC days a guy from the north-west named Kevin was desperate for a job. I rewarded him with the position of assistant exterminator, and he swore that if I ever came to Washington State he'd find me a place to stay. Happily, in the years that passed, Kevin had moved back to Seattle, and happily he wanted to make good on his word.

Fresh from Venice Beach, Bebe and I had $1,000 in our pockets when Kevin picked us up at the airport. Except for Kevin's new metal-head look (his shoulder-length hair gave him the appearance of a Guns N' Roses wannabe), the reunion was great, and we swapped old bug stories as we drove through Seattle. Even at night the urban centre was prettier than I'd expected. But then we kept driving and driving. 'Boy, this is a big city,' I said. It was then he informed me that he didn't exactly live in Seattle, but in the outskirts, a little town called Redmond. We drove some more and finally made a left turn into a long tree-lined driveway – as long as many thoroughfares, and bumpier than a rollercoaster.

He parked outside a shack with wood falling off. I ran to the door, swung it open and was greeted with a collective *Whinny neigh!* There were a dozen horses inside. 'Hey, Jesus,' Kevin said with a laugh, 'don't worry – your manger's upstairs.' I was relieved walking up those steps, until I got to the apartment on top and realized that all that separated us from the horses below was one thin plank of wood.

When I took a whiff of the country air that wafted through his abode, I realized, *Oh my God, we're gonna live in a horse barn!* We could see no evil but we could sure smell and hear it.

First thing Kevin did was show us our corner that we were allowed to occupy. The second thing he showed us was his new drum kit, which he loudly demonstrated.

Twenty-four hours later, in between drumbeats, I had discovered more about horses than I cared to know. I had learned in detail, from that thin piece of wood away, the noises horses make while relieving themselves, and how they nervously trot around breaking it up afterwards – increasing the smell threefold. I'd learned that in a horsehouse you had to breathe solely through your nose, or you could literally taste the horse shit.

But that was just the tip of the steamy pile. With nothing to do except pound his skins, Kevin had become more neurotic than I remembered. He was obsessed with a pinprick pore on his nose that he believed was crater-sized, and kept asking if he needed cosmetic surgery. When not talking of his pore, he fretted about his receding hairline, which the naked eye could not detect. And between his constant neuroses he was pounding, pounding, pounding on those drums and any other non-breathing object.

Between the horses underneath and Kevin on top, we were counting down the days before we could leave.

Luckily, we only had one week before Labor Day weekend, when the city's Bumbershoot Festival takes over the compound known as Seattle Center. First built for the World's Fair in 1962, the city centre that houses an amusement park, a science centre and the artefact of 60s futurism, the Space

Needle, is a mob scene over the three days when it becomes home to the multimedia shindig Bumbershoot. For that weekend the exhibit halls, arenas and grassy knolls spilled over with music, theatre, art shows and street performances, making it a cross between Vienna and Venice Beach. The place is screaming with creativity, from the high-brow to the strange, and you can guess at what end of the spectrum I fitted in.

Happily, unlike Venice Beach, it wasn't hard to find a space in the field of street performers. Thanks to a lottery system that designated spots, I didn't have to resort to fisticuffs or bribe someone to lay down a towel. My space was right next to a burly, bearded Renaissance man with a twinkle in his eye named Payne Fifield, who had a medieval magic act. Alas, our shows started at the same time. Due to my experience at reeling in a crowd, his small crowd was trampled. My crowd was much bigger and more receptive than the jaded southern California tourists. It was like fishing with a treble hook. The money poured in so easily, I kept looking over my shoulder for a game warden.

As soon as my show was over, Payne and I had one of those long talks like I'd tried to have those first days on Venice Beach. We struck a deal: I'd alternate times with his, if he would teach me how to stick my hand in a raccoon trap without coming out digitless – which was the only stunt he did that I cared to learn.

By my second show word of mouth was buzzing. I didn't have to look for a crowd, they were there waiting for me to start. I sensed that this was a city ripe for a new art movement, that there was an intrigue with these historical stunts. Seattle, after all, was a pretty hip place with a fertile subculture: bands

were sprouting up everywhere and, unsigned to major labels, they were still playing beaten-up local clubs where the booths were as weathered and ripped as the fashion. And throughout the underground scene lurked characters with tattoos, pierced eyebrows and studded tongues, people who followed Modern Primitives, who had a love of the macabre and may have even been into S&M. People who were into the underground and into shedding light on all that lurked in the dark.

And day after day at Bumbershoot they gathered around asking questions, from 'Where'd you learn that?' to 'When will you play again?'

The first question was easier to answer than the second. I didn't have a clue where to go from Bumbershoot. But I did have a new friend. Jim McConnell. He'd shown up at the second show, this guy with grey hair and grey eyes, who looked like he'd stepped out of a 1940s movie. He was one of those types that stand out so much, the rest of the crowd is a blur.

Afterwards he hung around, saying he was an actor in town. He convinced me that I had stage potential. For some reason I immediately trusted him – far more than the fat guy from Beverly Hills. This stranger was one of those generous artist-friendly artists. When he heard that we were living in a barn, he offered to share his house with Bebe and me until we got on our feet. I blew the last horse shit out of my nostrils and accepted. At last we were going to live in Seattle proper.

With his theatrical skills he gave me pointers on my new show, and he wanted no compensation. Having flown in to Seattle, I had ditched my bed of nails on the towel at Venice Beach, so Jim built me another one. It's the best bed I've ever had – and it's the one still used in the show today.

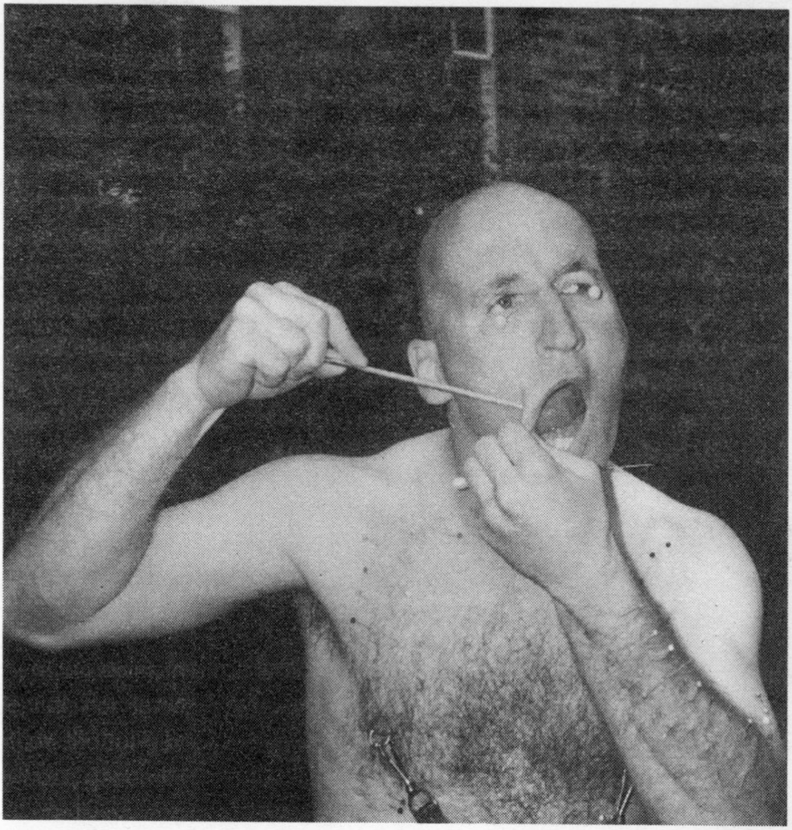

Scottish Pincushion.
Photo by Jim Rose

Lifto.
Photo by Mark Van-S, Seattle WA

This guy was a true pal – and my brain was oozing with confidence the day after Bumbershoot, when I headed out to the city to find me a geek job. With the reception I'd got at Bumbershoot I knew there was a demand; now I just had to find where to set up.

I went to every theatre, club and gallery, searching for a space to put on my show.

I went to COCA – an avant-garde gallery downtown, home to the wildest events Seattle had ever seen: acts like Survival Research Laboratory, with white-hot industrial machines that spewed fire, and the monster band Gwar, who wore elaborate sci-fi demon masks and squirted fake blood on the audience. But COCA declined. I went to other galleries, I talked with the owners of theatres – but no matter how delicately I described my act it sounded too gory. I went to the cool rock clubs like the Offramp, where bands such as Nirvana played. The managers listened to my spiel and invariably said, 'Uh-huh, that's nice. But what kind of music do you play?' It was dawning on me that Seattle was not a Welcome Wagon Headquarters. I kept hitting more venues, with the same response: 'You pound nails up your nose?' they'd ask. 'You eat light bulbs and throw your face in glass and have people stomp on your head?' Their eyes bulged, their faces went green and they looked at me as if I were trying to sell them pregnant lice.

Still, I kept badgering, I kept begging, until I ran out of money. I shoved aside my pride and took the only job that required performing: a phone sales job, signing up family portraits for Olan Mills.

I could sell eighty families a week on Olan Mills portraits, but I couldn't sell one person on my show. For six months I

tried. For six months I slunk home from every interview. And it would be another six months, apparently, before I could play again at the next Bumbershoot.

Bebe and I regularly dined at a small Middle Eastern restaurant called Ali Baba, a pitiful dive, truly one of the tackiest I've ever seen. Cheap tapestries were nailed to the walls and plastic Pepsi signs were stapled on top; there was a dinky stage in the back where belly dancers performed, typically only for the owners and their friends. The food was decent, though, and both Ali and Baba treated Bebe and me as if we were from a high caste – understandable given that we were the only customers. One night when I was crying over my baba ghanoush, Bebe tore off a piece of pitta bread and had a brainstorm. 'Why not do the show here?' I looked around the empty room, thinking that, if even eight people showed up, it would be eight people more than usual. The owners agreed.

Thinking that I'd probably be performing to one or two booths of the curious, I hastily stapled up posters all over town – featuring a picture of me lying on a bed of nails with three people standing on me. Live ON THE BELLY-DANCING STAGE OF THE ALI BABA , it said in huge print, THE MOST AMAZING ONE-MAN SHOW OF THE EXOTIC EVER OFFERED!

That Friday night I showed up two hours early to set up the stage – which was nothing more than a door on milk crates. When I walked in, the place was jammed: every booth and seat in the house was full. I thought Ali and Baba must be having a falafel special. Then I realized everybody was staring, at me. The place only holds a hundred, and two hours before showtime it was sold out. An hour later hundreds more pressed their noses against the window to see what was going on.

When I looked out into this audience, it was the underground nook-and-cranny crowd, the so-called alternative scene that would explode and put Seattle on the map eight months later.

These were downtown hipsters who could not be easily shaken. These were the art types I'd see in cafés and sleazy bars, that would never talk to me.

None the less, I expected interest. But I got more: Ohhs, Ahhs, bugged eyes – and my first faint, during the razor-blade munch. It scared the hell out of me. I stopped the show to make sure the fainter was all right. From that point on it clicked. I knew what this audience wanted. They were the Lost Generation – the ones who'd never seen sideshows that I, ten years older, had seen every summer. It was a virgin crowd, and I was in a deflowering mode.

And unlike my family-friendly performances at festivals, here I could be my typical manic, vulgar self. My show that night was raw, and I screamed 'Fuck' a lot. It felt so liberating. It was at this moment I married my job. It wasn't going to be easy, but with my personality it was what I was destined to do.

My Ali Baba act was a campy version of the Venice Beach show, with a few new stunts thrown in. Eating and putting cigarettes out on my tongue, hand in raccoon trap, walking up a ladder of razor-sharp swords, human dartboard, eating razor blades, human pincushion, stapling dollar to my face, eating glass, face-in-glass, nail up nose and bed of nails – but this time I had belly dancers, who pranced around waving scarves in between acts.

The next night the one-man multidancer show sold out again. After all I'd been through, I was more shocked than the audience. Perhaps my odyssey of the bizarre was going to pay off.

Matt the Tube.
Photo by Mark Van-S, Seattle WA

People started coming up to me, wanting to join up. 'I can cut myself up with a razor blade and bleed all over the stage,' they'd say, bright-eyed. And I'd say, 'You got it all wrong. If you can do that and not bleed, you'd be doing something different. I'm a big fan of Iggy Pop's – but that is not what we do.' I wanted professional circus performers, not mutilators. From that point on the line was drawn. No blood. At least not intentionally.

Seattle, so frosty weeks before, was suddenly thawing. Even though only two hundred downtown hipster sorts had seen the act that weekend, they got around a lot and kept stopping me on the street. Everybody said they'd been at the Ali Baba show. I was psyched.

But the heady zing of success was quickly squashed by a sick realization. The main man in a one-man show could only do so many stunts, pull off so many marvels, before people started saying, 'Oh, him. That guy. Yeah, saw him last month. Been there, did it, done it.'

There was a buzz about me after that weekend, but next week I could be salmon wrap. To keep that buzz I needed to showcase a revolving door of performers, a kaleidoscope of wonderment. So people would never know what to expect.

I needed something new.

And that something new came in the form of a car-insurance salesman with legs like a filly and a laugh that matched. His name was Joe. Back then, at least.

He'd turned out for the first show at Ali Baba, and came back the second, each time hanging around shyly while I gathered my gear. Tattoos, brandings and piercings were his obsessions; he'd pierced nine body parts, at home, without anaesthesia. The guy had balls, all right, one of the few body

parts that hadn't been pierced. Back then, at least.

After the first Ali Baba weekend he was onstage as the assistant's assistant, helping Bebe; before long he was part of the show. Joe, the car-insurance guy, had an act – lifting weights with pierced body parts – and a new name: the Amazing Mr Lifto.

I'd noticed another guy lurking in the audience, with dark hair and a dark look in his eye. His name was Tim Grimm. By night he was a movie projectionist; by day he was an information specialist. He even had an information-specialist act: he'd carry out two boxes, and then ask for questions from the audience. Whatever they asked for, he could find an article on that subject in one of those two boxes.

He rarely talked or smiled, showing his humour only when he explained his elaborate conspiracy theories: a question like 'Who turned on the light?' would elicit a long-winded rundown of unlikely suspects and improbable motives. He was a conspiracist who was on everyone's mailing list, and he lugged in a bag of junk mail every day. He said that he could do a more extreme human pincushion act. 'Yeah,' I said, 'but do you bleed?'

'Ninety per cent of the time, no.' It was close enough for me; he was the new Pincushion.

A few days later he brought his friend, Matt Crowley, a pharmacist who turned out to be one of the most fascinating people I'd ever met in my life. Tall, Nordic-looking and bald, he was a vastly intelligent man who'd read volumes on Houdini and had learned escape stunts, like how to get out of chains and handcuffs. Matt also had one of the most outrageous party tricks I'd ever seen.

At the time he'd just moved from Montana, and had

found a way to melt through Seattle's glacial social setting and immediately make friends and influence people. There was a dive bar in the heart of downtown called the Frontier Room, where the drinks were strong, the patrons were stronger and the sight of flying tables and chairs was routine. Matt was prone to stride in – a noticeable presence before he even opened his mouth – and loudly boast that he'd bet he could down a quart of beer in thirty seconds. Through his nose.

Well, the partyers were always up for a sight, and Matt would pull out a clear cylinder with a pump and seven feet of clear rubber tubing attached. Then, as mouths dropped open, he'd thread the tubing through his nostril and snake it into his stomach, and then dump a quart of beer into the cylinder. Amid groans and yucks he'd plunge it into his stomach. Worse, he'd pull it back out again. It was a talent that left sphincter muscles kissing their chairs. He, too, signed up for the show.

Not only were people coming up to audition – they were walking up to me on the street and actually offering me gigs. The first was Café Sophie, a posh downtown restaurant, where we were offered a show the next week. But before that we had booked in a storefront at the University Street Fair, when a store offered to take out their window and allow us to perform elevated and with a microphone at that weekend's event. The fair is a three-day scaled-down version of Bumbershoot, when the city's festival lovers walk up and down one main strip – called the Ave – which shoots off the University of Washington. With not so much as a rehearsal we signed on.

As we were setting up, a sweet-faced, wholesome-looking kid came by, said he was Paul the Sword Swallower and

Slug the sword swallower.
Photo by Mark Van-S, Seattle WA

asked to perform in our show. He enlisted – with the agreement that I'd do all the talking, and he'd keep his mouth shut, except for the pertinent moment.

It was hardly a troupe at that point. But the response for our show in the glassless window was phenomenal. The second day we performed, there was such a buzz going that the place was mobbed. Nearly four thousand people showed up. They were scrambling over merchants' stands, standing on windowsills, hanging like monkeys from trees. And, having never seen anything like this before, they were going nuts. By mid-show there was such a roar that the police promptly surrounded us and demanded we leave.

We took full advantage of the police stoppage by announcing we'd be performing a full two-hour human demolition spectacular, that night and the next.

Café Sophie, an elegant velvet-streamed restaurant, was a former funeral home – and I was elated, having started at a dead Middle Eastern restaurant and ascending to a classy joint where they had once prepared the dead. The managers didn't know what they were getting into: the upscale environs seemed to contradict our brash act.

I was committed to a two-hour show and had to pull out all the stops. Payne Fifield agreed to put his hand in a raccoon trap. Pincushion said he'd put down his projector. Matt the Pharmacist said he'd stop selling drugs and would show up to nose-chug. Lifto would lift, Paul would swallow, Bebe would assist. And I would do my stunts – and emcee. The belly dancers were left at Ali Baba.

The show sold out both nights and the masses got their $5 worth. They were boggled, sickened, and the owners flipped – not fully expecting guys who pumped beer in and

out, stuck hooks through nipples, pins in cheeks. Anything anybody had heard the week before was now obsolete. We were suddenly big news – and the guy who'd booked the show at Café Sophie was fired.

After noticing that the people in my audience were the club-going types, I retried my case with the rock 'n' roll clubs, and we were booked at the Crocodile Café – a space that held three hundred people and had a real mike system and a real stage. I printed thousands of posters and plastered them on every telephone pole in the city.

It was incredible: the *Seattle Times* and local TV and radio stations turned out to see our sold-out show. We were finally playing in a venue that matched our audiences. All of a sudden we were actually being interviewed. We were invited on radio shows – but unlike the days when I was the Voice of the Intercom, the microphones now seemed frightening. We were stiff and unprofessional and nervous, but it felt good.

Tom Phalen of the *Times* was the first to sense an entertainment phenomenon, and threw us a front-page feature story with a huge colour photo. In the *Times* article I'd promised an illusionist, a juggler and a dwarf – all performers who'd auditioned the nights before and, after the interview, had been promptly hired.

The Crocodile was ecstatic and promptly booked four more circus shows. And we sold out every night, turning hundreds away.

We added an extra date, figuring it would be easy to sell out as well. Especially since I had promised the one-time-only Seattle appearance of the lovely contortionist Andrea, and the bullwhippin', lassoin' cowboy Frank.

That night's show was magical. It was like a ten-ring

circus. Things were happening everywhere. Ropes were flying, hoops were twirling, traps were snapping – all at once. You needed a swivel for your neck.

But we barely sold out. And we were faced with our first crisis. Should we spend all of our days putting up thousands of posters in one city in the hope of luring those who hadn't already seen us? Or should we hit the road?

I held a big circus meeting. Everybody was there, from Dolly the Doll Lady, our advertised dwarf, to Jan Gregor, a man with a plan for Canada. I announced it was hazardous for our careers to be a uni-city troupe, and we should take time off while I put together a press kit that would garner shows around the world.

The question was: who would go? Some had jobs they refused to quit, some had children, some had bad attitudes, some had chronic car sickness. Everything had happened so fast, we didn't even know each other. The sifting process was gruelling. The list was finally drawn: the 1992 line-up for the Jim Rose Circus World Tour was Lifto, Paul the Sword Swallower, Matt the Tube, the Human Pincushion, Bebe and me. It was agreed that Jan Gregor would be our tour manager, if he could actually get us an on-the-road gig.

Jan came through: he lined up a Canadian tour with Frank Weipert. But it wasn't to start for two months. The freaks were getting restless, they were used to the limelight. We broke our vow not to do another Seattle show when we heard Katherine Dunn was coming to town. We were all fans of the author of the novel *Geek Love*, a cult classic about manufacturing sideshow freaks. The people bringing her to the University of Washington assured us that the prestigious author would not be interested in such base entertainment. But

the booker called back an hour later, in a puzzled tone, saying she'd be delighted to have us perform. We did the best-of version – all at the same time – and made a friend for life.

She invited us to Portland, saying we could stay at her house, and gave us numbers to call to set up shows. We took her up on her offer – and showed up the next month for two sold-out shows. That weekend Katherine had three floors of freaks staying in what she called 'the house the geek built'.

Afterwards we were climbing the walls, counting down the three weeks before we left for Canada. One day, while I was sharpening the ladder of swords, the phone rang.

On the line, a *Newsweek* stringer by the name of Melissa Rossi. A voice like hers had to be connected to a body that was tall, thin and voluptuous. She said she'd been hearing about us all over town and tales of our circus had ruined her recent dinner parties, and added that she wanted to pitch a story for a flashy front section of *Newsweek* called 'Periscope'.

I was elated. Our first national press. Even my parents would see this. Things were looking up.

Until I met Ms Rossi. Voluptuous, maybe. Definitely a squat: she looked as if God had hit her over the head with a big hammer. We met for an interview over dinner, which lasted until the wee hours of the morning. I did my best to stay on guard, but her humour was disarming and we quickly fell into bantering reminiscent of the days when I'd performed the Daily Bulletin with friends in high school. I nicknamed her Malicious Snotzi, which was a misnomer, because she was ridiculously sweet.

She called the next week and my jaw dropped: she said

Newsweek was going to run the story. She called back the week after that and my jaw dropped again: she said *Newsweek* was not going to run the story.

So close, so far. I was massively depressed – not to mention embarrassed. I had called every third cousin three times with the news. Now they were calling me bullshit.

But I didn't have much time to dwell on the fact that I'd be the laughing stock of the next family reunion. Because the next day we headed north to Vancouver. Paul the Sword Swallower showed up with jars of squirming maggots, worms and crickets. When I enquired if they were his travelling pals, he said, 'Change my name to Slug the Insectivore. I'm eating these.' I was revolted, and said 'OK, sure.'

Ah, the Canadian tour with the unforgettable Montreal show and the mayor of Toronto, who was pictured with the caption *'I am repulsed!!!'* next to a frightening photo of me saying, *'We are not monsters!!!'* Crammed in a van, creating controversy everywhere we went. Two weeks into it I called Rossi. She said the *Newsweek* item had come out after all. Knowing that we had nothing lined up after Canada, and crucially needing an agent to book a US tour, I called my answering machine, praying that someone important had read the article. Two had: Sally Jessy Raphael and Geraldo. We had offers to appear on both shows. There was a hitch: neither would let us do both. So we had to choose. We picked Sally – because Sally cares.

We halted our tour and flew to New York. When we arrived on the set of the NBC network, they had us wait in a green room with a lady for the next day's show, who had hacked off her cancerous breast to save on hospital bills. Even we were taken aback.

We demonstrated our stunts during a 'walk-through' for the producers. To fill up a full hour they wanted us to do every act, except for Lifto's penis swing, and Matt was not allowed near his tube. Even after nixing those two stunts they were taking bets on how long Sally would last before walking off. They wanted to put a happy face on our show, and had decorated the set with festive balloons and streamers, playing up the circus angle.

Sally, a true professional, soldiered her way through the first fifteen minutes – asking us questions and shoving her mike at the audience. The only person who said anything negative was a woman I'd seen taking coffee in the green room. I'm not going to come out and say it, but if I didn't know any better I'd have thought they had plants in the crowd.

And then we got to the good stuff. Sally declined our offer to feed glass to Pincushion, and ran to a corner where she stayed for the remainder of the show; every so often the camera would pan to Sally, looking faint and covering her eyes while we ran amok. Slug ate bugs. Pincushion stuck needles in his cheek. Lifto lifted irons from his nipples. I took darts in the back.

The remote controls of fickle viewers seemed to stick on Sally.

It turned out to be one of her highest-rated shows. Twenty million people worldwide tuned in that day.

As soon as we flew back to resume our tour, I called my message machine, certain that an agent was salivating. I got better news. *Entertainment Tonight* wanted to tape us. Fortune was smiling on us, because this show would be great for our career. After being on *ET* we could pick any agent we wanted. The *ET* theme played over and over in my head.

We met the crew in Montreal, where we returned on the second half of our tour. *ET* flew more people in than Sally had in her studio. Cameramen, sound men, producers, assistant producers, assistants to the assistants. They shot us from more angles than a prism; they occupied our entire day with interviews, make-up, more interviews, run-through, close-ups, action shots. It was tedious, exhausting, and though I was glad they were there I couldn't wait until they left, which they did the next day. I was told they spent $40,000 on production to tape us that day. Clearly *ET* intended to make the circus huuuuge.

Jim Rose and Perry Farrell.
Photo by Danny Clinch, 1992

PRESS BEGETS PRESS

The day the head producer of *Entertainment Tonight* saw the tape from Canada, I nearly cried. So did he. 'There's not three seconds of this we could show on national television' was the message handed down to me. No agent had called. There was nothing to do. I was back at square one, because we couldn't even play in our home town.

The Canadian tour was over, and we were too. Oh, sure, I'd made grand promises to the troupe that the next tour we'd have a bus, but I now knew in my gut that we'd never get a bus, because we'd never tour again. We were washed-up has-beens who'd hit the heights when we were on *Sally Jessy Raphael*, bless her wimpy little heart. At least she'd had the balls to put us on the air. We'd saturated the Seattle market, the Portland market, the Canadian market. With no future tours booked, no club greeting us with open arms and no immediate income, our only career direction was down, down, down.

I had a bad case of the back-home-again blues. Anyone who tours knows the syndrome: even if you're complaining the whole time on the road, dreaming of nothing but your own bed, it's anticlimactic returning home; you suffer a postpartum withdrawal, where you miss the roar of the crowds, the hum of the bus motor and even get all misty-eyed about the driver.

But it was more than just that; there was legitimate cause for concern: whereas bands can kick back and collect royalties from their records, and authors can relax after a book tour waiting for more printings, we had nothing coming in. And I had a weekly payroll going out. I'd persuaded everyone to quit their jobs, and if I didn't toss out the bucks they were going to quit mine.

I became despondent, and every time I'd try to see the pluses and minuses of throwing in the hammer, only pluses lined up. I had a mind to just start up a termite-killing company. Given my foul mood, it was easy to come up with a name: Bug Off.

Sometimes, usually when my heart had been warmed by a particularly touching episode of *Murder, She Wrote*, I had a faint glimmer of hope. I tried to convince myself that things weren't as dismal as they seemed to me, when I looked at my calendar and saw that every single box was white. We did at least have a marketing tool: a promotional tape.

And what a piece of work – that twenty-minute videotape from Canadian shows, pieced together on a shoestring budget, illuminated with less than professional lighting and guided by a kind-hearted but inept cameraman prone to forget he was supposed to sweep through the audience and not just zoom in on one of the audience members' breasts. But a tape that none the less captured the horror in the eyes, the fainting, the puking

– and the sickening sights onstage that were eliciting those effects.

Knowing it had the same likelihood of reaching its desired target as an Iraqi missile, I placed the tape in the hands of everybody I knew from street musicians to club owners to Susan Silver and Kelly Curtis, managers of Soundgarden and Pearl Jam respectively. That tape was shuffled from hand to hand, finally ending up in the four of Perry Farrell and Ted Gardner.

And at that particular moment those four hands were the most beautiful hands in the world. Because Farrell, former headman for Jane's Addiction, and Gardner, his manager, had a project that I wanted to be part of.

Something they called Lollapalooza.

Lollapalooza. God, I loved the way the word drooled off the tongue. Even more, I liked the concept: Lolla being the most awesome musical display since Woodstock (the Real One), except this one rolled right into your town. A roving rock 'n' roll city, the nation's only annual music festival, a monster party on wheels roaring across the country and looking for a place to call home for a night.

I'd first heard of it the year before while busking and basking on Venice Beach. I never thought that maybe someday we might be invited.

When I read the roster for Lollapalooza '92, it seemed that temperatures, religion and harvest themes dominated the bill. Headliners Red Hot Chili Peppers would play on the same stage that was warmed up by Ice Cube, the Jesus and Mary Chain would be passing the basket to Ministry, Lush would ready the ground for Soundgarden and Pearl Jam.

I was yanking my own chain, pulling my own leg, even to

pray that we'd rate a bench in their league. Besides, most of the time I was so filled with gloom that I didn't even have the nerve to dream. The thought shoved to the back of my mind, I continued with my twenty-four-hour mope-a-thon.

Then, one day, after what seemed like three years of anxiety but was actually nine days, the phone finally rang. It was Tube. It had to be Tube, playing yet another prank. Then it dawned on me it wasn't him on the line. It was actually Lollapalooza – saying they wanted to enlist us. Two months on the road, forty shows. They expected fifteen thousand kids to turn out for each one.

Turned out the call wasn't a crank or even a wrong number. It was totally legit. And that day was the happiest day of my life. Except, of course, for the one when I met Bebe.

Granted, it wasn't like we were playing between Soundgarden and Pearl Jam, and it wasn't like we were even playing on the main stage. But it wasn't like I cared.

I would have gone as a roadie's shoeshine boy. I foggily agreed to all terms offered, as one thought dominated my brain, beating through my veins, jolting every cell: We're going on Lollapalooza! We're fucking going on Lollapalooza! Fucking fuck, we are going on Lollapalooza! It was the beginning of a manic fucking high that would last many fucking years.

Hours later the phone was ringing again. This time it was *Spin* magazine. Perry Farrell was flying up to Seattle the next day, and they wanted us to do a photo shoot with him.

So Perry came to town for about three hours, but in that short time he was a whirling dervish in front of the camera, revving us up like a cheerleader, and every time right before the camera clicked he yelled, 'Come on, tense your neck, do

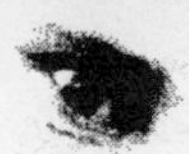

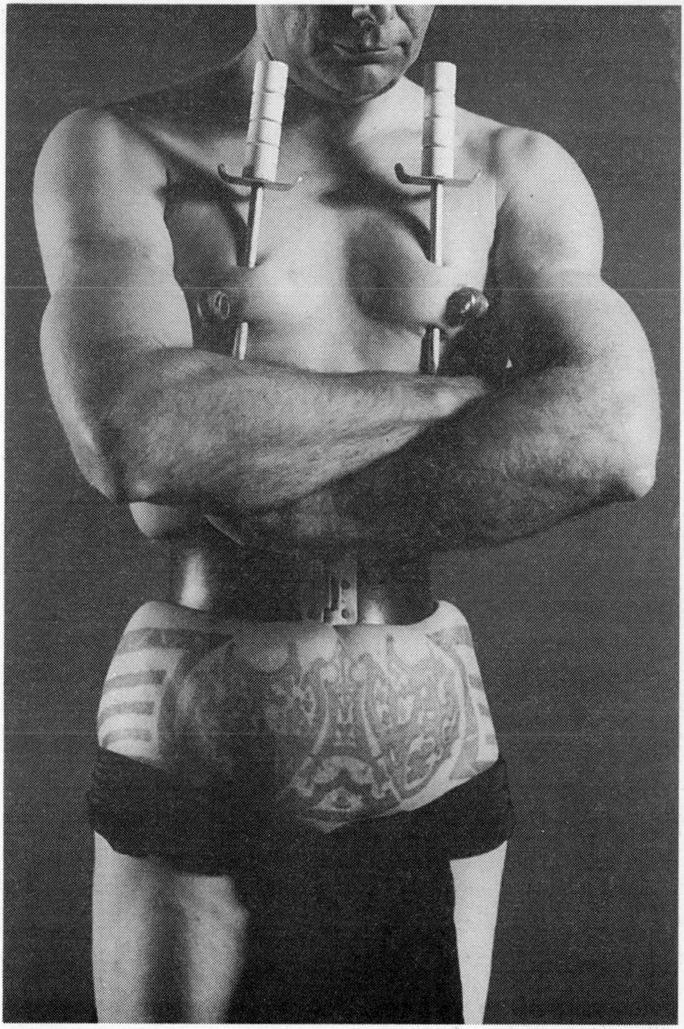

Fakir Musafar.
Photo by Roland Loomis

some faces, COME ON, IT'S THE COVER!' We hopped roof to roof with photographer Danny Clinch, an image genius who did covers for *Spin*, and wailed on the harmonica for Blind Melon as well. Then we hit the Crocodile Café, filled with ripped-open booths and a fibreglass tornado whirling from the ceiling, and took more shots there. What can I say? It was unbelievable that we, the goofy little troupe, would be pictured with Perry Farrell in *Spin*. By the end of that shoot we would have marched with Perry anywhere. There was a big buzz going in gossip circles – everybody knew Farrell was in town, and they knew why, and our message machine was lit up like an 0898 number on Valentine's Day.

I didn't have time to return all the calls, because one particular call was taking up all my attention. It was a call from the *Nose*, my best-known organ of childhood. In this case, though, it was a snotty magazine out of San Francisco that runs anything irreverent, from which celebrities forgot their scorched spoons in the bathrooms of posh restaurants to who was last seen passed out and drooling in small-town tavs. Being the daring sorts they are, the *Nose* wanted to sponsor us for a two-day kick-off for Lolla.

So this time we pointed the compass south, towards the Golden Gate Bridge. The magazine's publisher, a strapping young hipster by the name of Jack Bolware, is the sort who could be called the spotter, the attentive guy who gives first notice of the approaching locomotive; in the underground press he was something of a physician, attuned to the apoplectic pulsings of popular subculture.

I had been flattered when he called up, because the kiss of the *Nose* is the underground equivalent of Betty Crocker's seal of approval. But I got real tense right after Jack swept us

to the DNA Lounge, a balconied club that reeks of subculture, filled with beaten-up couches that were three inches deep in grime and hipster hair. No club looks good with the lights on, but this one looked like a whorehouse on dollar day. But that wasn't why I was worried.

There was good reason for my tension: this was San Francisco, and we were just a bunch of freaks who hadn't even played California before. And it dawned on me that in a place with as fertile an underground scene as that city's, we'd probably bomb.

San Francisco is home to Fakir Musafar – the king of the Modern Primitives, who invented the term and owns the trademark. This was the capital of branding and body-piercing and the dark S&M scene. It was the headquarters of Survival Research Laboratory, mad industrial scientists who create and destroy technological wastelands right there onstage. These acts were hard-core. San Francisco took its art seriously. The subculturati were thick-skinned and hard to shock. And here we come to town joking and laughing, the happy Rocky Horror Freak Show. I envisioned the calloused subculturals hissing, 'Boring,' 'Stupid,' 'This sucks!' and throwing Rice-A-Roni at our heads.

And, since the place was swarming with press who were in town waiting for Lolla, our gutless, soon-to-bomb act (or so I assured myself) would be skewered in newspapers nationwide. We'd be twirling on the media's rotisserie before Lolla even started up. Realizing we were losers, Lolla would boot us from the show. The scenario ran through my head like a continuing nightmare.

Since the press was there, I took everything I had studied, from Barnum to Ripley, from Houdini to Howard Stern, from

Evel Kneivel to Don King, not to mention Alice Cooper, and, fuelled by sheer anxiety, I worked on making every interview an event.

I crunched light bulbs on radio stations, I chased cameramen with chains and handcuffs, I'd show up for interviews with Matt the Tube, who had a hundred firecrackers taped to his bare skin, and he went off like Mount Krakatoa.

We were a human demolition spectacular! A circus of the scars! Not since Christians were fed to the lions has there been a show this dangerous! People are tired of things that are slick, contrived, choreographed, predictable and clean! The Jim Rose Circus gives it to you live, real, raw and dangerous!

I was a revved-up media machine in the classic circus tradition. But deep down inside I was, am and always will be worried. We'd talked the best game we could. Now we had to perform.

We were incredibly nervous backstage, but were at least distracted by what had become a ritual: Slug could never figure out a good cricket security system. The sight of him on all fours backstage, slapping cupped hands on the floor, always dictated our starting time. We couldn't start until he had caught enough of the runaways for a hearty insectimeal. Finally he'd caught his dinner, and with a tremor in my stomach and a fear in my heart I strode on to the stage of the DNA Lounge, scouting out appropriate escape hatches for when we were booed.

Turns out I was just being paranoid. Before long I saw that familiar horrified, sickened look in the eyes and heard the well-known moans and groans; it was obvious we must be doing something right. Especially when seven people – including a nose-pierced punk in the front row – passed out

during the first act. Pincushion really got them when he poked the needle in his eye. That was a real faint-jerker.

Backstage after the show, the mood was disgustingly giddy. I could hardly keep back those sickening Sally Field sentiments: 'They liked us, they really liked us.' Thankfully I did, because suddenly there was a series of knocks at the door.

Knock One was Chinese delivery. Knock Two was the Baron – a shrivelled old-timer, as weathered as Plymouth Rock and nearly as old. He'd been a sideshow guy in the 40s who blew fire, and, though he declined our offer of moo shu pork, he nibbled on some of Slug's creepy crawlers, and noted that the ants tasted like pepper. Opening his mouth, that wrinkly hole under his nose, he went on to shove in more creepy crawlers, proclaiming, 'And these live slugs are the freshest of sushi!'

Knock Three was the Holey King himself: Fakir Musafar. He was a personal god to Mr Lifto, who was acting like he was in Shangri-la. A middle-aged guy with short dark hair, glasses and a no-nonsense demeanour, except for the porcupine quill rammed through his nose, Musafar looked like what, as a former ad exec, he in fact had been – your typical uptight suburban businessman.

Until he took off his suit (which he soon did). Underneath those clothes he was a work of art, adorned with primitive tattoos and symmetrical piercings. The holes and slits dotting and slashing his skin were used as sheaths and holsters; once swords and daggers were inserted, he looked like a family coat of arms.

I'd read so much about him, heard so much about him, seen so many odd pictures that even I, who am rarely at a loss

for words, was dumbfounded. Finally, my voice kicked in and I asked the only question worthy of such a holey man: 'Do you mind, Musafar, if I stick my thumb through your nipple?' He didn't, and I did.

Of course, Lifto was shooting off questions and begged for a show, and the stunts began. With a deep breath the fakir tucked his organs under his rib cage and sucked in his stomach till his waist shrank to Scarlett O'Hara size (like the belle, Musafar kept his figure dainty by wearing corsets). With a deep breath the Baron rose from his chair, slugged a swig of lighter fluid and blew a huge fireball, nearly melting the swords in the fakir's skin. Lifto was in such hog heaven, he wasn't even rooting around in the groupie trough.

So between the *Nose* send-off and the next day's flurry of radio and magazine interviews, the tour was starting on an up note – but it would get higher and higher. From then on things just exploded.

Bebe the Circus Queen gets a melon chopped in half on the back of her neck.

Photo by Mark Nouillan

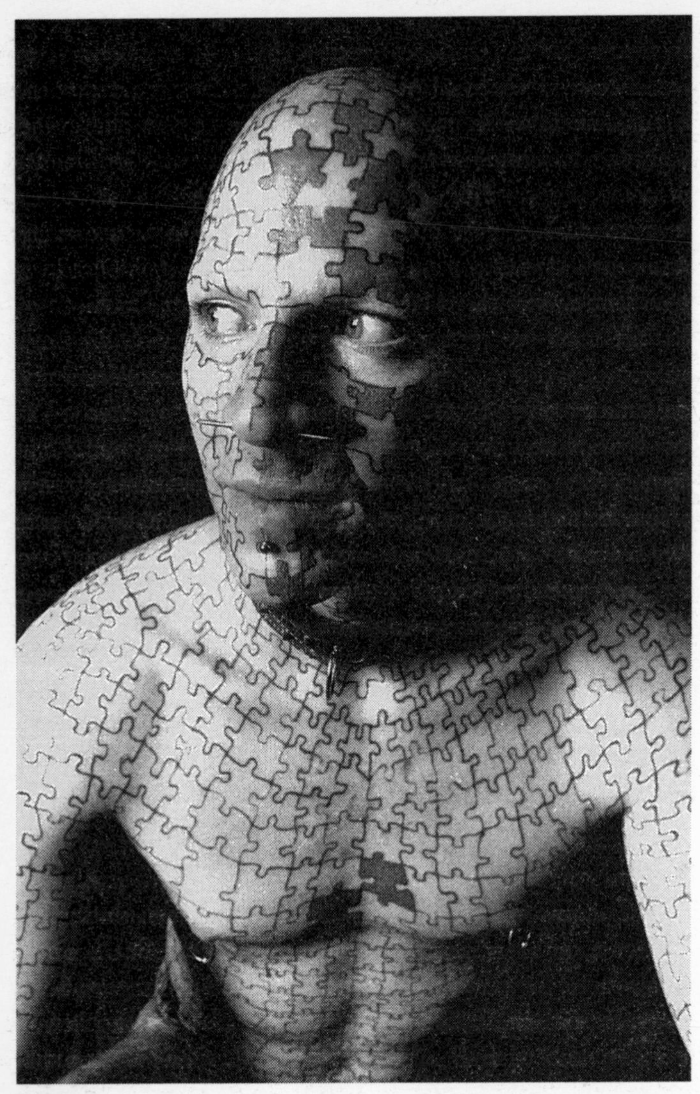

Enigma.
Photo by Alison Braun

ON THE ROAD WITH LOLLA

The day before it had been a field. Just a bunch of grass, with clusters of wild flowers swaying in the summer breeze, and bunnies hippity-hopping from rock to rock – a site so pastoral you could imagine cows swishing flies while chewing the cud. But then Hurricane Lolla touched down.

Suddenly, the place was a jumble of wires, security, guitars and beautiful girls, a swirl of boxes flying, and construction guys rigging, digging and ducking.

Speakers and scaffolding towered above the stage, which was a snakepit of buzzing electrical generators and crackling coiled cords. It was an executioner's dream. Roadies tarzaned from platform to platform, avoiding the death zones underneath, putting on more spine-tingling performances than any high-wire or trapeze acts. Banners and posters were nailed across stages or tacked to the back of latrines, instruments were being shuttled from trucks, speakers hoisted and stacked. And everywhere microphones were being shoved into faces.

All the big-name reporters had flown to San Francisco for the first day of Lollapalooza, and all battled for the inside scoop; if the rock stars weren't talking, they interviewed roadies, parking attendants, caterers and the guys on dollies.

Lollapalooza, by definition, is an all-day sucker. When applied to the festival where seven bands overtook the main stage, it's music that lasts all day and is good to the last lick. But for me Lollapalooza was Latin for 'heaven'. I'd never been involved in so lavish and classy a production.

The opening day at Shoreline Amphitheatre, outside San Francisco, there was a heady zing in the air. The minute we stepped on to the field, we got an instant inkling of how wild this tour was going to be. Bill Graham Presents was behind the San Francisco show, and the company is known for making life really sweet. For the send-off they'd gone all out: the sprawling backstage was packed, brimming with velvet chairs, antique mirrors and overstuffed couches littered with glitterati. The dressing rooms were bigger than horse barns I've lived in, filled with ping-pong tables and pool tables and video games; mounds of food were piled high and the alcohol flowed freely.

The city's Cool Ones turned out for the event and were swarming around everywhere. Bands had their contingents of friends, who'd brought contingents of friends. Everywhere we looked there was somebody who had been on the cover of *People* or *Rolling Stone*. And the press was swooping down from all corners, flashbulbs were blinding and cameras were rolling.

Those cameras were often pointing at us, due in no small part to our total availability. Unlike most of the stars, we were not exactly hard to get. Also, unbeknown to us, Heidi Robinson, one of the best rock publicists in the US, had pushed our circus

as a featured act. Suddenly, wherever we went, media from New York, Europe, Australia and Japan were right behind, picking up our trail. We loved it. Let's face it – we were not shy. At any given moment, at the slightest provocation, Lifto was showing off his Prince Albert, or Slug was swallowing a cue stick, or Cush was chomping on a glass.

We were not just hamming it up for the press; we were laying it on for the bands. Everybody hung out in the main dining room backstage – simply called 'catering'. Amid the pizzas and tacos there was lots of handshaking and backslapping as the bands met each other, many for the first time.

Since we were instrument-illiterate, and hardly knew a Fender Mustang from a Ford, bands quickly dropped their musical chat and asked us to eat bugs.

But of all the musicians backstage none stuck out as much as Al Jourgensen, hard-rocking Ministry's bad boy. Very bad boy. A giant of a man, with goatee and black dreads streaming out from under a cowboy hat with the brim pinched down. He looked like the leader of the toughest biker gang, this lead singer and heavy-metal guitarist who had earned the nickname Buck Satan. The first time I saw Al, he was heading for the stage with a fifth of Bushmills whisky in his hand, taking big slugs off it. He was very staggery. None the less, he looked like the type that you wouldn't want to fuck with. Some guys get so drunk that, even if they're eight feet tall, you know you could kick their ass. But he gave the impression that the drunker he was, the meaner he was. Making you want to stay away from his ass. The backstage was a riot, hanging out with guys from Soundgarden and Pearl Jam – Chris Cornell, Eddie Vedder, Jeff Ament and Kim Thayil. We'd never met them

before, but being from Seattle they knew who we were (and vice versa) and we shared a civic bond. That night MTV cornered Pearl Jam, and we got an unexpected endorsement when Jeff, the bass player, yelled out, 'You've got to see the Jim Rose Circus Sideshow!'

You wouldn't have noticed our new-found notoriety, however, if you were reading the schedule of events: we weren't listed. Only the main-stage acts made the ads and posters. We were playing the second stage, a fraction of the size of the main stage, and located so far across the field that you needed a Weed Eater and alligator repellent to get there.

There on the second stage is where we met Sharkbait, a seven-piece industrial band out of San Francisco who put on a wild show: they played springs and huge barrels, and were audience-interactive, handing out drumsticks to pound on washing machines, refrigerators and television sets that were scattered throughout the field. The grand finale of their beating ceremony was when they left the stage, pounding all the while, and pied-pipered the audience a hundred feet away to the Rhythm Beast. It was a huge monkey-bar structure with sheet metal, bumpers and hubcaps bolted on that people tried to beat in unison with a sledgehammer. If you were pounding the Beast, it felt like you were in a groove, one with your neighbour; but if you were walking towards the metal contraption, it just sounded like a hellish racket. Sharkbait wound up their set by getting everyone to scream, in between bangs, 'We love you 'cause you never stop crushing.'

And then it was our turn to take over the stage. The crowd was sweaty and revved up, all two hundred of them. I looked out across the audience, and had eye contact with each and every one and wondered, *Where the fuck are all the people?*

Our part of the field felt vacant. But about half-way through the show we were up to a thousand people. Near the end, when Matt the Tube was emptying his stomach, the crowd had built to two thousand.

Granted, that was the biggest audience we'd ever played to, but two thousand out of seventeen thousand people didn't seem like a very big piece of the pie. Everyone assured me we were doing well, but it just didn't seem good enough.

But what could we expect? We were in a desolate corner playing against Soundgarden, who were on the main stage. That's where the other fifteen thousand were hanging. Given the choice, I would have done the same thing. I was a huge Soundgarden fan, so much so that I'd listened to the first fifteen minutes of their set before I ran across the field to do my own.

We were caught between a rock band and a hard-rock place. Not only were we playing against Soundgarden; since we weren't listed on the schedule, it wasn't even obvious we were playing. We were on Lollapalooza, but nobody except the press knew it.

When I asked the heads of Bill Graham Presents for pointers on getting a bigger crowd, they suggested that we come on twenty minutes later – after Soundgarden ended, during the change-over when the stage was dead. With nothing happening on the main stage, lookie-loos were out in full force, milling around on the field, taking in the art, the banners, the hair braiders.

Now I just had to figure out how to make our stage a magnet. The next night before the show I recalled the barkers I used to see at the Arizona State Fair.

As soon as Soundgarden finished, a voice boomed across the field and the main stage. 'Will the Human Dartboard

please report to the second stage,' it said stiffly. 'The Jim Rose Circus Sideshow is about to begin. Human Dartboard please return to the stage.' This was followed by muffled panicky pleas. 'Has anybody seen the Human Dartboard! Is he drunk again? Somebody find him!'

A few seconds later the official voice boomed back over the speakers. 'Attention: all ambulance, paramedics and police please report to the second stage. The Jim Rose Sideshow is about to begin.'

Of course it was me, hidden behind the curtain like the Wizard of Oz.

People started pouring across the field to the second stage, murmuring about the Human Dartboard, but I wasn't satisfied yet. Once they were in, I talked very softly into the mike, in a nervous nice guy's voice, the kind you'd expect from the resident electrician. 'Hey, everybody that can hear me,' I whispered, 'please listen. We're having a problem here. Before we can start the show we need your help to check the monitors. When I count to three, please scream at the top of your lungs and take three steps forward. Are you ready? One, two, three.'

Everybody walking by heard the screaming, and saw people swarming the stage. We had found our magnet. That night eight thousand people came to the show; our chunk of the field could fit no more. They were vacuum-packed in so tightly and pressed against the stage, they couldn't have left if they'd wanted to. The air hung with a sauna-like heat. People had been partying all day. And we were doing stunts at an eye-popping pace, bam, bam, bam. Due to the heat, drinking and smoking, we were overloading their eyes. The fainting began. That night we counted more than twenty, bam, bam, bam.

Susan Olsen, the former Cindy Brady of *The Brady Bunch*, saw the show and was quoted as saying, 'I laughed, I cried, I threw up.' She was clearly up close. The stage was so low most people couldn't even see the stunts, but they stayed anyway – pulled in by the descriptions and the eerie keyboards.

And after that night's show the change was obvious, just in the way people followed us. At first it seemed to be my imagination. Out of the corner of my eye I could see people running after us as we walked across the field to catering. But when I stopped and looked behind me, the people I'd thought were following me froze; then they acted like they were just walking along, whistling. And when I started walking again, they started running again. But the next time I turned around, they didn't even try to hide it. They were swarming us for autographs. We were getting mobbed, chased around, our name was yelled out in waves. It was beautiful and amazing, the kind of hoopla that many bands come to hate.

That night after dinner we saw it. Oh, happy day. Our bus. That's right: we got a bus. We finally got a bus. A bus that was a palace on wheels.

The bus had a dining room with a TV, VCR, CD player. It had a kitchen with a TV, VCR, CD player, refrigerator and microwave. It had a bathroom that you couldn't shit in, but we didn't know that yet. It was nothing short of heavenly. And I couldn't wait to hit the road. San Francisco was over. Our next stop: Vancouver, British Columbia.

As we climbed on, my silent celebration of finally having snagged a bus came to a screeching halt. It suddenly hit me: our palace on wheels would house more than me and Bebe, it was home to even more than just the eight-person troupe. It

would be filled to the gills with fifteen people. Because Sharkbait was more than just a band with whom we shared the second stage. They were our busmates.

I quickly did maths. Fifteen people, two TVs, two CD players, two VCRs, one microwave. Fifteen people, one bathroom. Suddenly our palace seemed as grand as a pup tent.

That night as we piled on to the bus, about to pull out for

Al Jourgensen drinking bile.

an eighteen-hour road trip to Canada, I immediately detected two problems.

One was the sleeping arrangements. There were only twelve bunks – a situation that throughout the tour meant that

some people would be forced to double up, and some would have to sleep on the table. I decided not to be one of them and claimed a mid-bunk as my own.

Shortly after that I discovered the second problem: Rusty. Our booze-reeking bus driver, with coarse red hair like a bunch of gnarled wire coiled around his head and an alcoholic bloat that made him look like he was forty-five going on Social Security. Rusty was a madman, and drove the bus as if he was Greyhound's answer to Mario Andretti. Perhaps for good reason, since I was soon to learn he always showed up late. We were invariably the caboose trying to catch up with the train. And since his breath was invariably blasting whisky, his driving wasn't winning any smoothness awards. Every time he rounded a curve, there would be a collective *ka-thunk* as a half-dozen bodies were thrown out of bunks. From the first night on, the sound of bodies being tossed around was as common as the hum of the refrigerator, and choruses of 'Oh, Jesus' and 'Who gave this guy keys?' echoed through the night.

For the first stop on the Lolla road tour – Vancouver – we roared in almost half a day late. Rusty showed up crocked and had to take a pre-drive nap, and we were the very last bus to pull out.

We were, however, only the next-to-last bus pulling in Canada. Ministry's bus was the very last to arrive. Guess they encountered a few problems about the second they roared on to the freeway. About the second, that is, that Al Jourgensen exploded a few bottle rockets, and they ricocheted through the aisle of the smoke-filled bus, blinding the driver and forcing him to jerk off the road. The driver promptly kicked them out

and drove to the next rest stop, where he called the police. Ministry was real late that day.

As I stumbled out of the bus, in a fog from the sleepless night – Rusty driving with the finesse of a five-year-old who's stolen his parents' car keys – the reality of this party-on-the-road dawned on me. Rome wasn't built in a day. But Lollapalooza was. And it fell the same day. Everywhere across the field I heard hammers pounding and saws sinking their teeth into wood and the morning sky was filled with the auditory ebb and flow of power tools raging and whining. Dust filled the air, creaky wheels were stuck in mudholes, and there were tape and cords everywhere as stages and tents were hastily assembled.

Meanwhile, hundreds of vendors pulled in to set up. It was a loose-knit caravan of hot-dog vendors, smart-drink pushers, hair beaders, temporary tattooers and people pushing many a political cause. They willy-nillied it across the country, some in cars, some in vans pulling trailers with kitchens inside, some working out a Greyhound schedule, to get to Lolla early and erect their booths.

Still groggy and aching from the many times my body had been hurled at high speed into the bus wall, I suddenly found a list of official Lolla duties in my hand, the details of which I hazily recalled having agreed to weeks before. It was a long list – and it began with: 8 a.m.: Assemble Rhythm Beast.

From there followed so many other feats of manual labour that I felt I was reliving a day in the life of Ivan Denisovich upon his arrival at Gulag camp.

I balked at the thought that my roadieless performers – forced to assemble (and disassemble) the stage for our act,

and then perform death-defying stunts on it – should be subjected to this additional manual labour. Plus I doubted that anyone could awaken them at that early hour. I sure didn't want to be the one to try.

So I quickly pulled aside management and tried to escape from the knots I'd previously tied us into. We were such a surprise hit those first two days, they agreed to let us skip out on our duties. From then on others were hired to show up at 6 a.m. to pick up the slack, and the numerous pieces of the Rhythm Beast.

Freed from our early-morning duties, we arrived typically at eleven to watch the final touches and polishings before they threw open the gates. Once the gates opened, at 1 p.m., none of that behind-the-scenes tetchiness could be detected. It was a small miracle each and every day.

Had Bebe and I been planning the tour's itinerary, we couldn't have asked for a more ideal city than Vancouver to start out in. Since we'd played there only a month before, there was that third-generation buzz: friends telling friends – hell, the Mayor of Toronto was still head-spinning in Linda Blair fashion from our last visit. Not only was Lolla a smash; our show was packed, an absolute madhouse.

Everyone was amazed at the turn-out, including Ted Gardner and Perry Farrell. Granted, we'd already established ourselves in Canada. But since the official impression was skewed in our favour, we weren't letting on.

Ted Gardner and Perry Farrell had gone all out to ensure that Lollapalooza remained free of corporate taint. Gardner, a barrel-chested Australian with a crewcut and a golden ring in his ear, looked faintly piratical. All the more that day when he

shimmied up a twenty-foot pole with a knife in his mouth to slash a Pepsi banner erected by local promoters. No one even tried after that.

He was widely known as Cap'n Ted, the cheerleader who rode around in a golf cart a-whompin' and a-whoopin', giving instructions to everyone on site. His everyday conversation was peppered with Down-Underisms like 'Good on ya, mate' (Australian for 'Thank you') and (in response to 'How are you?') 'No dramas.'

The next stop was Seattle – where, alongside Soundgarden and Pearl Jam, we returned as war heroes, although we'd only been gone for a week. We were going gangbusters.

Until we pulled into Colorado. San Francisco, Vancouver and Seattle were cities we'd trailblazed prior to Lollapalooza. Denver didn't have a clue who we were. Even with stealthy Wizard of Oz enticements, only three thousand showed up, though it seemed like three compared to the crowds everywhere else.

It was clear we could do better. I was edgy. I could smell a new trend: the farther we moved from Seattle, the fewer people showed up.

When I peeked out and saw the crowd, I remembered yet another old street-performer lure. It relies on the idea that, if you put on a great show, people don't remember what pulled them in. So I tried it out that night. 'Free beer, there's free beer at the second stage!' I announced between calls for the Human Dartboard, police and paramedics. 'Free beer, free beer at the Jim Rose Show.' It wasn't a lie. We did hand out free beer during the show. Matt the Tube's bile beer, that is. Little did we know what hot shit bile beer would turn out to

be by the end of the tour. The crowd rose to 4,500, much less than when we played our home turf. We needed the press to hit immediately, or a stroke of good luck. The latter came through – in the form of Chris Cornell.

The next day, in St Louis, Chris asked me to introduce Soundgarden on the main stage. An honour that I didn't expect. So I ran on and bellowed, 'It's the official Lollapalooza wake-up call. Stand up, everybody, stand up, stand up.' When the masses were on their feet, I screamed, 'Because here comes Soundgarden!' The band killed, they ruled, the crowd went wild.

Midway, I left to set up our show – and an hour later, when I looked out at the crowd, there was a sea of people. We got an absolutely huge turn-out. I couldn't figure out why. But that night at catering I discovered the reason.

At the end of the Soundgarden set Cornell yelled into the mike, 'OK, everybody – let's go see the Jim Rose Show on the second stage.' That was the impetus behind the mob racing across the field. From then on, every night he did us that same favour; thanks to him we drew huge crowds wherever we went.

By then press was hitting all over the place. We'd snagged write-ups in *People, Time, Rolling Stone, Newsweek.* We were becoming the summer's feel-good freak show. *Rolling Stone* said we were the must-see event. The international press dubbed us the most bizarre shock circus ever. Even Al Jourgensen was looking at us with something resembling respect.

At this point our backstage was as crowded as catering. The rock stars took us under their wings and treated us like little brothers. The camaraderie was intoxicating; invitations to

after-show soirées, pool parties and nightcaps abounded. We were bonded for life. Everyone knew that 1992 was special, the year when the underground crawled up and saw its shadows. It was the spring of a new era. Lollapalooza was the alternative kids' coming-out party, their generation's Woodstock. A passing of the torch was taking place; people were turning up their nose at the heavy-metal dinosaurs, flipping off the rock establishment. Radio and MTV would never be the same. Programming changed for ever that summer. From rock stars to food flippers, we all knew this was unique, and that we were all a part of pop-culture history.

That was even before we started sharing bodily fluids.

Yes, there was a new event on Lollapalooza. And it took place on our stage. Once again, Chris Cornell was the instigator. We were playing Kansas when it started, and boredom must have driven him to it. That night in the middle of our show, while I was pumping Matt the Tube's stomach, Chris strode out on the stage, took the mike and said something to the effect of 'I sure am thirsty. Might I try the vile bile?'

The crowd went ballistic, as he guzzled a whole quart. The liquid was green; others were green with envy or nausea. Fans and performers alike queued up to sample the frothy mix. That's right, dear reader, they were chugging vomit. I was amazed.

But not half as much as with what happened after that. The next night Eddie Vedder took our stage, and slurped back a litre. Al Jourgensen, realizing that he couldn't be first, decided to make up for it in quantity. The next night he tossed back two quarts, and asked for more. What he didn't realize was Eddie was gonna challenge him. The war was on.

In fact, the topic that sprang to everyone's lips, daily,

nightly, in catering, over drinks, was bile beer. Long debates ensued, always boiling down to 'Would you or wouldn't you?' While the others talked, Eddie did. By outdoing Al the very next night, when he chugged two quarts as well; but Eddie, as he was quick to point out, had drunk it before. Al countered by returning the next night and equalling the score. They called a truce and contemplated their next move, freeing up spots for others to participate in vomit-clean-up duty. There was no shortage of lip sponges. Micki of Lush, Flea of Red Hot Chili Peppers drank, and Gibby of the Butthole Surfers flew in for a special sip. At this point they were all more daring than me; there and then I vowed never to drink that shit.

By three weeks into the tour, after losing all inhibitions and dignity, we were getting used to life on the bus. Granted, there were always problems. The air-conditioning broke during the first heatwave, and it leaked across the bus floor. Rather than fixing it or giving us life preservers, Rusty had the solution: affix Velcro to the bottom of cups under the drips, so regardless of how wildly he took curves the drip container remained upright.

As much as we tried to instil order, people were always bumping into each other and sliding over things, kicking into the overflowing Velcro cups that littered the soggy floor. It felt like we were in a rolling can of elbows and assholes, all of them wet. On particularly windy and bumpy roads the refrigerator would fly open, and it became a deli in a hurricane, with meat flapping, food flying, USDA hell.

The bus, luxurious though it had seemed at first glance, was inflicting nearly as much wear and tear on the body as was our show, especially with crusty Rusty scraping the wheels. Despite its advantage in roominess over a van, it

carried more people: the per-cubic-inch value was about the same, and each day on the road was a search for comfort wedged between people whom we now knew better than kin. Every square inch of one another's bodies had been seen at some time or another; we all knew too well each other's bodily quirks. At every rest stop, during those moments that before had seemed so private, conversations echoed from stall to stall; on days when noises weren't made by mouths, you could recognize who was there by the shoes.

Back on the bus, the tall suffered the most disadvantages and backache from the bunk system, where all stations – high, middle or low – were equally undesirable. The bottom bunk was loud and vibrated due to being closest to the engine, the top bunk was hard to get into or out of, and the middle bunk was a conversation sandwich, less noisy than the bottom but more annoying. Despite the curtains around every bed, you could always hear people screwing or snoring or hacking through the night. But we never complained too loudly around Sharkbait, who were rotating naps in the kitchen.

The living room in the back was the smokers' quarters, where the conversation was better if you didn't mind the second-hand smoke and the smouldering of the heaping piles of butts, source of many an ashtray fire.

But there were always attempts to homey it up: Lifto taped up posters from rock mags over his bunk and on the refrigerator was a grizzled picture of Al – with assorted wounds and scars drawn in, as if he needed them. Every night we'd hear the familiar clattering of Pincushion's needles boiling on the stove, and Tube would lock himself in the bathroom, performing his secret tube-sterilization ritual to which no one else was privy. Many a night we spent gathered around the

video watching racy and disgusting flicks that were passed along bus to bus, or listening to underground prank phone-call tapes like *The Jerky Boys* and *The Tube Bar* long before their CD releases. In short, it was hell but we loved it.

But into all good times a wrench must be thrown. And that wrench came in the form of the 'Who shat on the Bus?' mystery. Now this was a classic, the kind that they should have brought in Jessica – or at least Columbo or Matlock – to solve.

From the first day on the road all bands were duly informed of the intricacies of their buses.

Our mystery began shortly after Rusty was canned and a new driver, a southerner who went by the name of JR, took his seat. JR was a good old boy from Georgia with a moustache, cowboy boots and belt with a gleaming silver buckle, and an unbelievably good nature. Rusty was a drunk; JR was a pro. One morning after we awoke, he pulled the bus over to a rest stop and called a meeting.

'Boys,' he said sombrely, 'last night, well, somebody shat on the bus.' He paused to emphasize the gravity of the situation. 'Now, boys, you're not supposed to shit on the bus. I know who did it, but since we haven't been over the ground rules for the bus, I'm going to talk to them privately.'

By this time we were mid-tour. We were bus-broken and knew the rules: you can't blow up bottle rockets, you can't take your favourite groupie on the road, you can't accumulate a bunch of junk. But the cardinal rule was you can't shit on the bus. It goes into the tanks and seeps back into the bus via the vents and stinks the whole place up. The warning NO SOLIDS was posted on every rest-room door.

Granted, Al Jourgensen supposedly shat on his bus, paying the bus driver an extra cleaning fee for the privilege,

Jim Rose pumping a solution down Matt the Tube.
Photo by Michael J. Spilotro

but everyone else complied with the dictate.

The jokes soon began, with everybody saying, 'Hey, I saw JR talking to you - so you must be the shitter!' But nobody would cop to the crime.

And by the second day it had become an obsession, with everybody pointing fingers at everyone else. By the third day the only thing anybody talked about was Who Shat on the Bus? and conspiracy theories were ripping rapport to shreds. The Freaks were starting to call Sharkbait 'Sharkshit', the band was starting to call us the Lollapalooza Shitshow.

I hastily called a meeting with Sharkbait and all the Freaks to get to the bottom of the mystery. It quickly became apparent, as each person was questioned, that whoever had done it was a great bluffer: nobody looked guilty, there was no telltale twitching or blinking, no stuttering or tear-filled eyes. So we resorted to more hostile methods, and the dining-room area became a pit of loud arguments and accusations, with alibis flying and alibis reviewed and re-reviewed.

Finally I yelled up, 'Come on, JR, who did it?' And JR yelled back, 'I'm not going to embarrass him. But the shitter isn't in Sharkbait!'

So Sharkshit was back to -bait and proudly left the table, vindicated. Meanwhile I confronted my own men, and things heated up again. It could have been Pincushion, taking a conspiracy crap. It could have been Lifto, whose thin body wouldn't hold food long enough to wait for the rest stop. It could have been Slug having to pass a cricket urgently. And they, of course, thought it could have been me, taking a power shit.

The only one who had a solid alibi was Tube, who'd been partying in Soundgarden's bus. Pincushion protested that Tube had committed the perfect crime, crawling in through

Lifto with a coat hanger through his nose.
Photo by David Harradine

the vents, shitting and running back to the other bus; Cush, after all, was a guy who bought books just to read between the lines. Over his loud protests Tube was dismissed as unlikely. Suddenly fingers started pointing at Bebe, who seemed on the verge of tears as accusations swirled.

JR, eavesdropping from the front, quickly cleared her of wrong-doing. 'And it wasn't,' he yelled back, 'a woman!' This left Cush, Lifto, Slug and me. By this point every examination technique had been exhausted, all areas covered, all alibis subjected to microscopic review.

We quickly broke into factions – Slug and I drilling Lifto and Pincushion, and Lifto and Cush drilling us, while Slug and I winked all the while, saying, 'We know who did it.'

The debate carried on into the night, with everyone swearing and swearing it wasn't him. By dawn he who shitted had not admitted. Weary from fighting, we called a truce. So the person who fouled the bus was never publicly exposed. But Slug and I know who it was; we're just not telling. We don't want to embarrass Lifto like that.

But we weren't forced to sleep on buses throughout the tour; three or four times a week we had the luxury of a hotel. Upon arrival in whatever city we were to play next, we checked into hotels in the boonies, since the parking lot had to fit twelve buses. With nothing to do for miles we typically packed the hotel bar, along with most of the bands and the VIPs, leaving the staff plenty to talk about for weeks to come. And that was before they saw the way the rooms were left.

Musicians are notoriously rough on their rooms. By mid-tour, when nerves were grating and egos were rubbing, many of those rooms were out of control, sometimes from rockin' after-hours bashes, sometimes from rock-star tantrums; in either

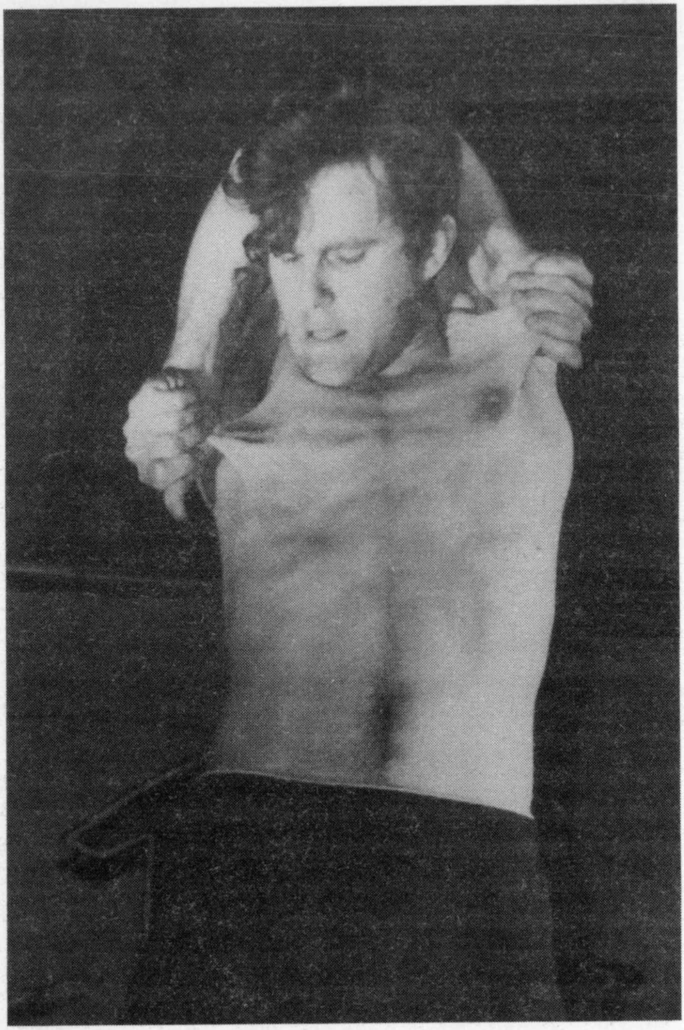

Rubberman caressing himself.
Photo by Bebe Rose

case anything can happen. Especially Ministry: Al was the king of the trashers. He and his heavy-metal cohorts were always setting off the sprinkler systems, forcing evacuations all through the night. At four in the morning he'd head out on an alcohol run, pounding door to door and loudly enquiring, 'Ya got any whisky?' Al didn't care whether he was waking up Lolla guests or tourists who'd had the misfortune to land on his floor.

And when a rock star has a hissy, pedestrians should watch out. One night as I was leaving our hotel in New Orleans, I heard a window break and looked up to see a high-speed TV coming toward me. I jumped out of the way, but it landed so dangerously close that shards of glass whizzed by my head like wasps.

Looking up I couldn't tell from which room the TV had been air-mailed, so I just yelled, 'Hey, Al, switch to decaff!' and went on my merry way.

By mid-tour the manic high had become routine, and we sought new ways to amuse ourselves. Eyes soon turned to the golf carts that security, managers and the worker ants used as their chariots. It started when Mike McCready of Pearl Jam broke his leg. Recalling full well from Arizona how to hot-wire the things, I jumped into a cart and, with security people chasing me, roared off to give him a lift. We'd go around dressing rooms honking the horn and offering rides to assorted musicians. Pretty soon they learned to hot-wire the carts themselves, and the field was filled with bumper cars.

The golf cart was the original bond between Eddie Vedder and me. Backstage, Eddie looked out of place among all the glitz and bimbos. He stuck me as pure, a guy with his

ego in check who loved to talk to real people. Before the gates opened, we'd drive out into the parking lot and stop to talk to small pockets of fans. Eddie could talk with the common man for hours, and was in his element when he was telling them his problems and listening to theirs. Watching him I got the impression that not only does he touch people, they touch him. A true rock Gandhi.

Meanwhile Lolla's Lucifer, Al Jourgensen, never cared to learn how to hot-wire. When he wanted to go somewhere, he'd simply wave a cart down, shove the driver out and pirate the vehicle.

The last thing I wanted to do was race by dressing rooms and risk being cartjacked by Jourgensen. So instead I drove the carts to an Al-free area: amid the general public. Specifically, the Porta Potti village, which was wrapped about by a long line of people shifting weight foot to toot, and tapping nervous fingers on folded arms, waiting for the keys to the city. Just for laughs, with megaphone in hand, I'd skirt the crowd and, in an official voice through a megaphone, warn, 'Attention, please, the blueish chemical that smells like antiseptic in the bottom of the Porta Pottis is highly flammable. No smoking in the Porta Pottis, please. We've had two vaginas and a penis catch on fire already today!' People would start cracking up at that one. Then I'd boom back, 'Don't laugh, sir – it could have been your vagina!' People weren't sure if it was a public-service announcement or what, but all smoking materials were quickly extinguished.

The fun behind the wheel was stopped abruptly when threats of a fine were posted all through catering. Everyone quit, except for Al Jourgensen, who considered a $50 fine a fair price for an all-day cart with unlimited mileage.

Meanwhile Lolla was covering more ground than kudzu. I had to find new ways to amuse myself at every stop. Watching a city being erected in literally hours fascinated me, and I took on week-long projects trying to learn about the different wheels of the Lolla machine.

One week I'd hang out with security; the next with promoters; the next with the caterers or the guys who hawked T-shirts. The week I spent with the roadies was perhaps the most insightful. They're a different breed, late to bed, early to rise – somehow surviving on two and three hours of sleep. The pay is good, but money alone can't buy that kind of all-day hard labour. What, for some, makes the job tolerable are its perks: free booze and free love.

It wasn't the promoters, agents or rock stars who got the most girls, because all roads to the stars begin with the roadies. They're a high-testosterone bunch who are the first to arrive on site and the last to leave, giving them first (and final) dibs on the groupies who strut a chain-link fence away. As holders of the most backstage passes, roadies are the toll bridge, and they do take their toll. Knowing it's the early bird that gets the worm, a groupie day plan is to dress scantily, get there quick and shake, shake, shake, giving good girls a bad name.

Maybe it's the long hours, the sleep deprivation or the plethora of women, but roadies have the jaded gallows-like humour you'd hear in a prison. My last day hanging around them, they taught me the secret roadie code.

If it's wet, drink it.
If it's green, smoke it.
If it's white, snort it.
If it moves, fuck it.

If it doesn't move, load it in the truck.

By then the coming and going of rock stars had become commonplace. On any given day you might see Steven Tyler, ZZ Top, Ice-T, the Butthole Surfers, Metallica – it was a virtual parade of the Best of *Spin*. But the day Al Jourgensen brought William Burroughs backstage, everyone went so completely silent you could hear a slug slither. Burroughs, considered by many the godfather of the underground, was the only sight that could shut people up. All were in awe.

He came walking towards me with long strides, a whirlwind of arms, legs and cane.

My first thought as I caught sight of his withered features was He looks so very, very, very old. My second thought was I've got to get out of his way. Because Burroughs doesn't seem to have a bum leg. That cane is sometimes used for leaning when he's standing, but it's always used for batting people out of the way when he's walking. When the cane was within millimetres of me, he suddenly stopped.

I became a quivery heap of nerves as he said, 'Jim Rose – I just saw you eat razor blades!' He'd apparently just caught our show. 'I saw a man in Tangier who did that,' Burroughs continued. 'He had two stomachs!'

And one of them was filled with bullshit, I thought. The razor-blade stunt doesn't require extra organs, but it seemed like a fond memory for Mr Burroughs, so I didn't want to crush it.

A while later we were talking about literature. I asked, 'What do you think about Louis-Ferdinand Céline?' Céline was my favourite writer, and I pulled closer to hear the praise Burroughs would no doubt heap on him.

Burroughs looked thoughtful, for but a second. 'He's

dead!' he said. I wasn't sure if he was making fun of me or what, but I appreciated the brevity.

In short, save for the occasional plummeting TV, life was sweet.

And except for the weather. It was one soggy summer. It rained, it poured, it hurricaned.

The day we pulled into Cleveland, one of our last dates, was a relief. It was a lovely summer day of the sort captured in Manet paintings. We frolicked and revelled as we basked in the sun. But an hour later a pregnant dark cloud rolled in and let it rip, putting an immediate end to our little game of tag. The rain slapped against faces and slammed against rickety booths that quickly toppled. It lashed out at the second stage, peeling off the roof and knocking the structure to splinters, sending us scurrying towards the bus. It packed a wallop and there were hot dogs, comic books and political pamphlets strewn everywhere.

Then, as quickly as it had hit, it departed. We couldn't do any more shows, but an hour later electricity was restored on the main stage, and then insanity broke loose. Because Pearl Jam came on, sucking people towards the stage like a vacuum. By this point of the tour they were huge. They'd leaped to the top of the charts, becoming the most popular touring rock 'n' roll act in the States.

Relieved that the show would continue, driven into a frenzy by the band before them, the fans went nuts, moshing and dancing and transforming the field into one giant mud pit. Games of mud broke out spontaneously: they were eating it, throwing it, wrestling in it, making slides that people waited in line for. By the time you slid to the bottom, you were completely

Al Jourgensen, William Burroughs and Jim Rose.
Photo by Lifto

covered and had mud in places that would take years to clean.

The backstage had taken a whipping. It was as muddy as everywhere else, and pocked with pools of liquid dirt.

Instead of avoiding them, Eddie and Chris dived in and took mud baths. If you consider yourself a regular person, there is a downside to fame: every time you walk out in public, you're mobbed. Eddie and Chris had been complaining about it for some time. And with the downpour they saw an opportunity for true anonymity.

Freshly dipped in nature's disguise, they ran out to the field and mingled with the general public, who had no clue

that they were mud-mucking with their idols. They stood in line at the mud slides, they played all the games, tossing mudballs and wrestling. Once again, mud proved to be liberating and the great equalizer.

This disaster in Cleveland was the most fun day on the tour.

On the way out all you could see was mud-people, throwing mud at every bus that passed. Tube had constructed a mask of Eddie Vedder from a life-size photo. And whenever anyone tossed a glob at our bus, Tube would hold the Eddie mask up to the window – and the mud balls stopped flying as fans chased the bus crying, 'Oh, Eddie – we didn't know it was you!'

At that point I got a hint of what daily life was for Eddie and Chris. I wouldn't want that kind of adulation hanging around my neck.

Finally, after eight weeks on the road, we pulled into Los Angeles for the last two shows of the tour. Worn out and road-rattled, I was starting to get antsy again. What the hell were we going to do next? Ever since the opening day I'd been followed by agents trying to sign me, some even lining up to chug bile beer as if that would win Brownie points – or greenie points, as the case might be.

With my eye on Europe I had to make a decision. Who would be the agent for the Jim Rose Circus? There in Los Angeles I got to meet in person a voice I'd only heard over the phone. John Branigan.

All the other agents were trying to impress me with whom they represented. Their plates seemed too full to dedicate much time to us. But this young Branigan, who'd just been promoted at William Morris, had fire in his eyes. The choice

was easy – especially after he said he could book us across Europe within six weeks. Oh, the power of William Morris. Later that day he introduced us to Mark Geiger, one of the powers behind Lollapalooza and a talent scout for American Recordings. Geiger promptly signed us to star in a full-length video of the circus.

With this bit of business behind us, relief set in and there was nothing left to do except kick butt for the finale. So we did. With the help of Eddie and Al again. By tour's end their bile battle had resumed. For the second-to-last show Eddie climbed on our stage – and defiantly downed another quart. He was ahead of Al again!

But for the final show Al clambered onstage and downed a quart himself, to even the score once again. That night backstage, the last night of Lollapalooza, there were tears and cheers dripping and clanging everywhere. Al And Eddie eyed each other, knowing the bile war was unwon and that there would never be a truce.

Eddie broke the silence. 'Al,' he said confidently, 'you're about to go on tour. But we're not. So I've got the time to hang around the Jim Rose Circus and drink bile beer every night if I want to.'

Al glared at him for a second, then shrugged. The last words I heard him mutter were 'Fuck it, then. I'll just make my own.'

Lollapalooza '92, the best summer of my life, was over. But we weren't. Branigan had booked us to do a private party for Ozzie Osbourne. We didn't know what to think about the former front man for Black Sabbath – rumours of his antics abounded. He'd supposedly bitten off the heads of live bats and rats onstage. Was a true rock legend going to enjoy our show?

The answer was NO. He sent his kids out of the room, and covered his eyes with his hands, only taking them off to shake mine on the way out.

On the way back to Seattle we were zonked. Hardly a word was spoken until we hit the Oregon border. Then, amid the snores of the freaks, Slug turned to me with a strange look. 'Jim,' he announced, 'I'm going to be blue.'

I immediately suggested Prozac. But Slug had something different in mind. He wanted to have blue jigsaw pieces tattooed all over his body. And he wanted a new name: the Enigma.

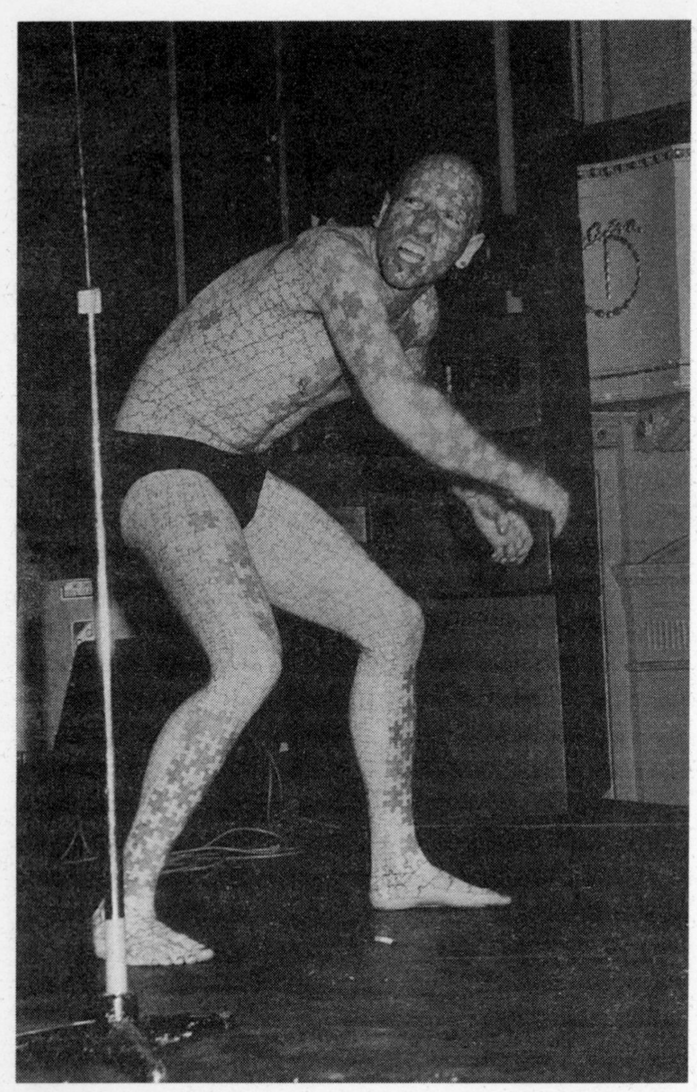

The Enigma acting surly.
Photo by David Harradine

EUROPEAN RAGE

The truth is that, once you hit the road, you don't remember the good shows. They're like every other show.

The ones that pop out like a throbbing haemorrhoid in your memory bank are the shows that were hell. And of all our really really bad gigs, none sticks out more than the French Fiasco – our first performance in Europe.

When Branigan called to say he'd booked us a European tour, I was ecstatic.

Europe. We were going to Europe. As a troupe. To storm across the land where it had all started for me – where I'd first seen someone stick his face in glass, and said, 'My life will not be complete until I can do that!'

Europe: the second continent that Barnum overtook, the next step for Houdini. Home of storybook architecture, church bells and town squares filled with performers – a land that looked like it had jumped out of Disney World!

We were going to Europe! I shouted the joyous news from street corners, my every waking moment filled with the

thought. There was a bounce in my step, a whistle on my lips, a Bavarian *oompah* in my heart. I nearly slapped myself to make sure I wasn't dreaming. But before I had a chance to, reality did it for me.

My manic high was short-lived, ending about the second we stepped into Seattle International Airport to start the big journey. A travelling freak show has enough problems crossing borders on wheels. But now we, who terrified and awed for a living, had to pass by tight-lipped international security, trying to convince them we were harmless.

Getting through the metal detector was a fresh new nightmare. Lifto, with his many ringed organs, was beeping from head to head. Bebe was French – that sent her into a different line altogether. Maybe it was the needle scars in his cheeks that formed dimples, giving him a perma-smile, or maybe it was the strange reading material, but Pincushion too drew stern, disconcerted looks.

But the one who popped and dropped the most jaws was the Enigma. True to his word, the Enigma, formerly Slug, had begun the enigmatization. In the six weeks prior to Europe he had gone through a tattoo-athon, putting in fifteen hours a day to transform himself into a world-class eccentric, showing a true commitment to sideshow.

Tattooed from shaven head to toe as a jigsaw puzzle, he now blurred the difference between man and monster. Marked for life! The Enigma was twenty-four years old. What was he going to do when he was sixty, looking like that?

It was only one of the questions going through the minds of sixty-year-old security guards, who eyed him as an international threat, through of unidentifiable ethnicity and species.

Every time we tried to walk through customs, we were

shuttled back to luggage check-in; apparently swords, nails and raccoon traps are not considered legitimate carry-on items, because God knows you might try to hijack a plane by clamping a raccoon trap on a pilot's head. It took hours to get everyone through.

Finally we settled in aboard a 747 amid the strange looks from fellow-passengers who were wondering how they'd got stuck in the freak section. And everything was great – for about, oh, seventy-four minutes.

Until a microscopic organism lodged somewhere in my digestive tract. Being sick is bad; being sick on a plane for eight hours is surreal. I spent most of it hunkered down in the bathroom, ignoring the desperate knocks and pleas of old women, small children and stewardesses. I never went back to my seat, spending the entire time in there. Even a direct order from the pilot could not have got me out.

When we arrived in lovely Rennes – where we were the first non-musical act to play at the prestigious Transmusicales Festival – I had no desire for croissants, café au lait or Bordeaux. Sick as a dog, I simply wanted to be taken to the local cemetery and buried. Instead I crashed out in the hotel, praying that tomorrow the organism within me would have jumped on to a new host.

My prayers were not answered.

The next day was hellish.

Although the festival promoters treated us royally, catering to our every whim, the problems were soon obvious: the production staff spoke only French, and Bebe was overwhelmed by a thousand questions flying her way.

Worse, while my stomach writhed in agony and I feared that any second my body would do something that would

quickly clear the room, I had to play meet-the-press. The European press viewed us as artists, instead of rock-'n'-roll freaks. They weren't content with questions like 'So where did you learn this stuff?' and 'How'd you guys meet?' Oh no. Their questions were along the lines of 'Is your performance true art? What historical significance does it have? How do you counter claims that your show is lewd and pornographic?' Very intellectual questions that I would have preferred to ponder at a moment when I wasn't plagued by the trots.

It was a nightmarish session; between my fever and their heated questions, sweat was dripping down my forehead, which gleamed as if under police lights, during this press conference that felt like a cross-examination. I explained what I could, excused myself from the room and never came back.

But the theme for the Rennes show was: things could get worse. And they did.

The micro-organism in my intestinal tract was subdividing and setting up a colony. I became so hideously sick that I spent the remaining three hours holed up in my dressing room, having another heart-to-heart with God. I'm not a religious man, but when you're that sick, God is the only one who isn't driven from the room.

Feeling weak and chilled backstage, I feared the worst, yet somehow, even with my imagination, I never imagined how bad the worst could be. Just as my name was called, I tried to negotiate a fart, but was losing. So I fought the fart. And the fart won. Thank God I was wearing boots.

I squished out to the microphone, and was hit by the full weight of our translation problems. My inkling became a reality. I talked slower and louder, but still could not communicate.

Enigma and Jim Rose waiting in the airport.
Photo by Bebe Rose

We'd never played to a crowd that couldn't understand English. Typically, the show starts with me finding an audience member and saying, 'You look like a jaded fuck – verify this is a real hammer and a real nail.'

That night I grappled for a translation. '*Vous blasé fuck!*' I said, pointing to a mean-looking sailor. '*Vérifiez, s'il vous plaît.*' Maybe my French was just real bad, or maybe the French have no sense of humour, but when I yelled it out the line, which usually gets the first nervous laugh that starts the show, got nothing. It just lay there in the stiff air like a corpse. Dead, dead silence – and the man at whom I was shoving my hammer and nail looked at me with terror.

So I grabbed my hammer and nail back, and pounded the nail up my nose. I'd done it thousands of times by then, but

that night the nail went up the wrong passage. Blood shot out. A Red Sea gushed from my nose. Someone finally handed me a piece of cotton wool the size of a mitten, which helped only slightly and made me look like an idiot with it hanging out of my nostril, flopping like a mop.

By now I was a madman, and wasn't acting. There was no way to humour them and take back the reins. This show was entirely out of control – and we were only five minutes into it. I was gushing blood from one orifice, something grosser from another, and the crowd was so sickened they were ready to bolt.

And then Lifto pranced out. Oh, a happy sight indeed. Since we were in France, this was the first place since Montreal that he could do his act nude. The feat of lifting irons with a penis did not require translation. Audience members' necks stretched as high as his penis stretched long, as they peered over the crowd for a closer look. During his act there were no mishaps, and he literally saved the show that night – buying us time between strokes of misfortune. He also bought me time to go behind the speaker cabinet and throw up some more of my flu.

Then the Enigma appeared for sword-swallowing – and I tried once again to ask a jaded fuck to verify it was a real sword. This time the jaded fuck actually grabbed it. But then the idiot just passed it back into the crowd – and the sword was swallowed up in the audience. It took ten minutes to get it back, during which time we were forced to stand there looking perplexed.

Next it was time for my face-in-glass act. Repressing the urge to puke again, I gestured to an audience member in the front row to come up onstage. And *voilà* – he understood.

Finally, the first person of the night was climbing up on the stage. Once he got onstage, he began crawling towards me. He was so drunk he could not stand up. Snot-flying drunk, he looked like a mad dog. I considered throwing a drumstick into the audience and saying, 'Fetch,' but I didn't know how to say it in French. So I had to walk him back into the audience. The crowd liked that impromptu act nearly as much as Lifto's penis-pull. I gestured at someone else, but he ran away. I gave up the hope of any interaction with this crowd, and asked Bebe to step on my head just so we could finally finish face-in-glass.

As if cursed, everything continued to go wrong: the French are apparently more delicate than I'd imagined, because when Tube did his tube they looked queasier than any crowd I'd ever seen. Minutes later what we had sensed and smelled was verified when Pincushion's electrical generator shorted and knocked out all the lights and sound in the building.

As we stood there in the darkness for ten minutes, a blanket of silence descended on the crowd, broken only by the sounds of intermittent puking and me fighting back another fart. Finally the lights came back on. Finally the hideous show was over, but not for Bebe, who'd invited all her relatives to our European debut.

And when we slunk out to take our bow, Bebe was sobbing her eyes out.

In short, it was awful, *très, très* awful.

But the fact that we sucked was lost in translation. The French press regarded it as artfully avant-garde and called me a dark angel. And the national paper *Libération* added that Bebe, upon returning to her homeland, was crying tears of joy.

So that's how we started our global march – with a show that was more a whimper than a bang. But on that unsteady foot we began a world tour that would employ us for most of the next few years. European tours were broken up by Australian tours, Canadian tours and US tours.

And after a while on the road it became a blur. Of foreign currencies and exchanges. Of strange plumbing. Of searching for a good burger in German villages or Swedish pancake houses.

All along the way Bebe, who'd become the circus business manager, served as our bank. Taking care of last-minute conversions when half the troupe forgot to change their currency, she was the expert on the foreign-exchange rate.

But each country has its own quirky characteristics and special stories. Each country has its own history of circus hoopla, and promoters literally scripted us into a variety of bizarre scenarios, each playing our hand in a different way. We always remember the really odd characters, the crazy bus drivers and the trauma-filled border crossings. And the only way to capture the insanity of our trek is country by country, starting with Great Britain.

GREAT BRITAIN

The fractured land-mass occupied by England, Wales, Scotland and Ireland is united only by a love of tea and ale, a bevy of easily excitable politicians, and the toughest borders in the world.

The border patrols of Jolly Old England are by far the worst. Maybe I'm being paranoid, but it seems as though they're set up bureaucratically and systematically to look out for Jim Rose, a name for them synonymous with moral decline and outrage.

Delays, detentions and deportations are invariably part of our import-export dance. The stone-cold faces, the stiff upper lips and the pregnant pauses between passport pages make you squirm as in no other country. 'So what is the purpose of your visit, Mr Rose?' they asked, their noses upturned, scrutinizing every stamp. Whatever my reply, a long silence followed, during which they considered any and every reason for shoving us back to wherever we'd come from. One time Lifto was nearly deported – because the back of his passport was filled with girls' phone numbers. 'This section of the passport, sir,' they sneered, 'is reserved for official use.' It's the kind of atmosphere where all the i's must be dotted and the t's must be crossed and your official paperwork should have been in years before your arrival.

The worst thing they ever did to us was to fabricate a small technicality on our work permits, forcing us back across the Channel to France, sending us to wait (and sleep) in a parking lot at the border in Calais. After receiving considerable pressure from several directions, they finally relented. Afterwards, *The Times* reported something to the effect that, 'Not since Lenny Bruce thirty years ago has an artist been harassed by our government like Jim Rose.'

The cause of all the consternation was a widely watched tabloid TV show called *The Word*. The most scandalous show on British television, it was known for shocking weekly. Three weeks before we arrived in Europe, *The Word* flew to Seattle to film us. They rented out the Crocodile Café and advertised a free show, so they could have crowd shots. The place was packed. The show aired live, being fed back to London and beamed to the English masses without editing. Lifto lifted irons with his penis, Cush stuck himself, Matt the Tube bile-beered,

and out of nowhere Eddie Vedder walked up and chugged the stuff, again. Putting him ahead of Al, may I add.

Penises, pins and Pearl Jam's leader drinking a cousin of vomit?!?! England was shocked! Appalled! Outraged! *The Word* received over six hundred complaints, the most in their history. The next day's newspaper editorials chastised the show for airing such lewdness and asked the readers, 'What are we going to do about the Jim Rose Circus, coming to town in a month?' One paper dubbed us 'the Sick Grunge Circus' – even though that's redundant. Before we'd even arrived we were a rip-roaring controversy complete with TV commentaries, articles and letters to the editor.

The tabloid machine was kicked into gear, and once those wheels are whirring there's nothing you can do to stop them. And if you're a circus trying to sell tickets in England, you don't want to stop them.

By the time our feet finally touched English soil again, the publicist greeted us with news that there'd been a 'a bit of a row'. Driving me to a press conference, he added, 'A few protests have been threatened, but they may not materialize. Don't worry, the tabloids will report them anyway.'

We pulled up to our hotel, the Bedford House, and there they were waiting for us. The TV crews, reporters and photographers – all wanting to be shocked, outraged and appalled! They don't care if you kill yourself – live! – as long as they get the exclusive. This was our first media event with the British press, and it was so organized and formal. They sat us behind a long table covered with white linen, asking us questions while the cameras flashed and rolled. We'd never been through anything like that before. They asked for demonstrations, so we lit up Tube, who'd been wrapped in

firecrackers, and they all ran out screaming – exactly the story they wanted.

The media there are completely different from ours. The English are a tabloid society, and every day what is paraded as news is a blend of soap opera and stretched fact. Tabloids feed on the English love of drama, and force issues down their throats, turning the most meaningless events into argumentative sagas, peppered with pithy quotes from both sides.

We had no idea the amount of controversy that *The Word* would generate. The English press wields a weighty sword, and is read all across Europe. Ducking in and out of government harassments, dodging opinionated outbursts from religious or conservative types while the press looked on, that was our constant daily drill all through 1993.

And wherever we went in the United Kingdom, we sold out shows. We ended the tour in Edinburgh – a gorgeous city filled with gold-lit storybook castles. Every summer they throw a three-week festival that brings in a hundred thousand Europeans daily with a choice of a thousand different events, from plays and operas to comedians and circuses, classical to fringe. It's billed as the oldest and most prestigious arts festival in the world, and we hastily agreed to a three-week run. Without time to advertise we needed a lucky break. It came in the shrunken form of a Conservative councillor.

So she showed up at our tent with a bevy of press, demanding that our show be shut down. Looking out of the flap, as cameras waited poised ready to shoot, and pencils were perched above paper, my publicist urged me to take advantage of the Kodak moment and give a token of peace. Alas, I'd forgotten all my keys to the city, so I had to make do with what was lying around. With much ado I presented her

with the official Jim Rose handcuffs that linked Seattle and Edinburgh together permanently. She was aghast! Cameras flashed; she was aghast! Again! The picture of me dangling handcuffs in front of that lady made front pages across the UK.

She was probably reaghasted when she read that all our shows sold out, making us the most-seen act of the entire fringe festival.

As much as I hate dealing with authority figures in the UK, on at least one occasion they've actually helped me. I might be wifeless without them. One time on the way from Britain to Holland, we pulled into a rest stop late at night. Most of the troupe was sleeping, and Lifto and I were in the back engrossed in another racy video. Minutes later, without much ado, the bus roared back on to the motorway.

We must have gone twenty miles when red lights began to flash behind us. The bus driver pulled over and, looking in his mirror, yelled back, 'Wow, they sure have good-looking cops here.' And then he looked back again and said, 'Uh-oh – it's Bebe.' Thinking Bebe was asleep, we'd left her behind at the rest stop. She'd run behind us for a mile in her stage garb – high heels, short skirt and fishnets – screaming and waving her toothbrush, still wet from the rinse. Luckily the cops had seen the Toothbrush-Waving Circus Queen and given her a high-speed ride. After that, we didn't leave so much as a hot-dog stand without taking roll-call.

HOLLAND

The beautiful land of windmills and tulips, home of Van Gogh and Rembrandt. The border patrol is never a problem going in, but you have to schedule an extra twelve hours for searches whenever you go out. Because Holland, particularly its main

cultural centre – Amsterdam – has a liberal view of sex and drugs.

It's got a red-light district, and hash houses dot the city, where, in between fresh fruit juices and shots of coffee, tourists smoke chunks of hash and roll joints of Maui Wowie.

But for us the most memorable moments of Holland were the impromptu stunts people demonstrated after shows. A guy came up in Rotterdam and said he could take a drag from a cigarette and blow the smoke out of his ear. I'd seen old sideshow posters of the stunt, but always thought it was a magic trick. He took a drag, and I peered intently in his ear, and was rewarded with enough smoke to cause cancer instantly. A huge plume puffed out.

I asked him how he did it and he said something about a broken eardrum. Apparently he'd had an ear infection and the drum never sealed up right. I was so impressed I invited him backstage, where he entertained the whole circus by taking a drag from his ear – and blowing it out of his mouth.

During intermission at the next night's Amsterdam show there was a knock on the dressing-room door, and Lifto opened it. There stood a beautiful brunette, whom he let in – and quickly requested an extended intermission. The brunette called herself 'the Candle Lady' and said she blew fire between her legs.

Now, this was something even I had never heard of before. The troupe gathered around as she shed her clothes and reclined on a table. While on her back she flipped her legs over her head, stuck a candle in her vagina, asked for someone to light it. She then took a swig of gasoline, and blew a huge fireball between her legs. The plume created more heat than a candle is used to, making it melt rapidly and form a

natural pool of wax around her anus. We all clapped, and when she stood up I heard a ping on the floor. I looked down and there lay a perfect wax imprint of her sphincter. I could have made a key.

Making the key for the nether regions was a lot easier than finding the key to get out of the Netherlands. You never get hassled in Holland, where anything goes. And all the other countries' border patrols know it. They're set up like armed camps, just waiting for you to exercise your new-found freedom in their country.

FRANCE

The French: their love of life is legendary. The aperitifs, the long lunches, the six-week vacations, the *je ne sais quoi*. They've got a laid-back attitude and find amusement in everything; rather than try to intimidate you like the British officials, their trick is to befriend you, making everything feel cheery and casual as they probe your innermost body parts. Their border guards are the most curious people in the world. And the most consistent.

Going into France means a free show, regardless of the hour. The badged patrolmen run aboard the bus with the glee of schoolboys on a treasure hunt. And then they start searching, holding up the raccoon traps to the colleagues, even duelling with the swords. And then they find the bugs. 'What do you do with these?' they say *très* officially. And we say, 'Oh, we eat them.' Then they start clamouring, 'Show us, show us, show us!!' After that everything they find they hold up. 'What's this for?' followed by 'Show us, show us, show us!' So we are literally coerced into putting on a show, show, show, in the parking lot. One night it was so dark, one of them held up a

flashlight while I lay on the bed of nails, letting them take turns standing on me – as Lifto stretched, Cush stuck and Tube put a condom over his head. But the grand finale is always when they pull that head-to-toe tattoo we call the Enigma into their office. Every single time he gets strip-searched. The reason: they want to see if his dick is tattooed too. (Once he became the Enigma only his girlfriend and the French border patrol knew for sure.)

Our last requirement is to give them dozens of T-shirts. Then they flash us a smile, and we're free to go.

Once in the country they don't care what we do or say, or if we're wearing any clothes when we do or say it. And though the French have treated us royally, wherever we've played from Provence to Paris, we've always left with the feeling that they didn't really get us. *Je ne sais quoi.*

BELGIUM

The country is a strange hodge-podge of its neighbours, friendly to many currencies and languages, but not to the Jim Rose Circus.

It all started as a nice friendly visit to a quaint festival in a small canal city called Ghent. We were scheduled to open a long week with few shows in a beautiful castle. We planned to spend it kicking back and resting up for Germany. All at the expense of the Belgian government.

Our plans quickly went awry. Starting the minute the Mayor read the latest English press about us.

While we'd been in Holland and France, the English tabloids had taken on a life of their own, portraying the circus as dangerous and reckless. With no regard to facts, news reports were flashing around Europe. There was the story of

my being pulled over and given a DWI, but I'd got off because we could prove my seeming drunkenness was the result of the lighter fuel I swallowed to blow fireballs.

There was the story of the animal-rights activist who had got into a fistfight with Enigma for eating crickets. The tabloid said Enigma won because 'HE BITES!!'

But the most involved and outrageous of the tabloid tales were the stories of our relationship with Super Glue. We did have a Super Glue act, in which Tube cemented a bowling ball to his hand. The tabloids had taken us to task by manufacturing a woman from France who claimed her daughter had come home from a show and promptly Super-Glued a tennis ball to their cat. Armed with that information, they had supposedly called the Super Glue company, which unleashed a litany of warnings about product misuse and abuse. They had me responding that the glue had been invented to seal wounds quickly in Vietnam – 'It's more skin-friendly than you think! The Super Glue company should sponsor us! We are showing consumers a new use of this product!'

From that generation of stories more absurd ones were built, culminating in the entirely fabricated tale wherein we'd glued the Tube to a cross in his underwear and hoisted him to the ceiling, testing out the ad in which they lift a man in a hard hat and fly him around dangling from a helicopter. According to the report, Tube had fallen off, leaving patches of skin on the cross and knocking him unconscious.

Armed with these reports and gorier rumours of what we actually did, the Mayor promptly booted us out of the castle and banned us from the festival. A patron of the arts from Brussels came down to rescue us, and we spent the rest of our time outside the festival boundaries, performing to sold-out

shows, living and sleeping in our new castle: an abandoned skating rink.

We'd trekked the bulk of Europe, taking the crowds by storm in the countries where English was, if not a first, then at least a second language: England, Wales, Ireland, Scotland, Holland and even (against the Mayor's will) Belgium. We'd been disappointed in Germany, Switzerland and even in France. But with all those countries we knew what to expect. For our last leg of the tour we didn't have a clue.

SCANDINAVIA

What looks like a three-pronged penis and a testicle to the untrained eye is actually a set of diverse countries – Norway, Sweden and Finland, with Denmark hanging off a little to the left. In general they don't enjoy being likened to one another. They are all, however, similar in two ways: their residents are the most gorgeous in the world, blond, blue-eyed and buxom – even the guys – and their ancestors were Vikings. But they pronounce the V as a W – so it's Wikings.

And that Wiking spirit still pops out of their genes. Given the warrior blood and the brutal cold (so chilling that it felt like each breath freezer-burned my lungs, causing all the tar to crystallize into black stalactites), the audiences were the most pagan I'd ever seen.

Not that the craziness was apparent initially. Our first Scandinavian show was in Oslo, and we were booked at the Opera House. Hours before our arrival we got word via fax. The Opera Society (having also read the English press) was having a conniption, and banned us from playing there. I saw a once-in-a-lifetime opportunity to amuse myself and faxed

back, 'My lawyers are looking into this matter, but it ain't over till the fat lady sings.'

But forget the cultured side of Scandinavia with which we nearly brushed hands. The Wiking country we saw in clubs and at festivals was debased and revolting in ways that made our most disgusting bus antics seem like the innocent merry-making of tots.

We started at the Roskilde Festival in Denmark. The site was crammed with seventy thousand people, all of them wandering among four stages and a tent. It was mayhem: everywhere we looked, the huge Wikings were dumping the Porta Pottis on their heads and flinging themselves like muddy dogs at the crowds. Unlike Lollapalooza, it wasn't mud.

From the first night on it was clear we were misunderstood. The promoter had billed us as the most disgusting act in the world, and dared Scandinavia to gross us out.

In some cities the fans would show up with more pins in them than Cush. Some would slash themselves with glass and be dripping blood. Some showed up on leashes and their friends would beat them. I don't know what the hell they thought we were, but it made even our iron-stomached troupe sick, and I'm not even telling you the most heinous stories. It was our saddest misunderstanding, and I haven't got over it to this day.

It came to a head with our last performance. The last show of the European tour. We'd travelled many miles for many months, enduring bannings, non-translatable jokes and cavity searches. Two-thirds of our final performance was spent weathering the glass hailstorm of flying bottles from the audience. I was getting ticked but, with only ten minutes left in our European tour, I was not about to stop our show. I didn't have to – they stopped it for me.

In the middle of the Tube's bile act, two muscle-bound Wikings, bigger than any bouncer, staggered onstage and took over our show. They yanked the tube out of Tube's nostrils, and grabbed the cylinder that held his still-frothing bile as it was coming out of his nose. And as if bile beer wasn't disgusting enough on its own, they peed in it. Then they drank some of it, and threw the remainder at the audience.

The bouncers cowered in the corner, and the circus, hardened veterans that we were, just looked in shock at the ongoing Wiking spectacle. With a shrug we walked off the stage.

Still dumbfounded, we returned to our hotel and tried to forget the nightmare. The next morning, boarding the bus, we came on the scene of yet another: all of our clothes were strewn across the floor, boxes were ripped open, trunks left hanging by a hinge. And almost all of our equipment was gone. Someone had broken in and stolen almost everything, except for the bed of nails.

On the plane back to the US I once again felt sick, but this time not for any microbiological reason. That Scandinavian tour had made me realize something had to change.

Jim Rose playing chainsaw football.
Photo by Danny Clinch, 1994

NEW CIRCUS

Something had happened while we were overseas. I saw it in the troupe's eyes. And I saw it in the newspapers and on the TV.

A British tabloid story had sailed across the Atlantic, and was getting big play in the United States. At least this one was partially based on truth. While in London I'd been asked repeatedly one day to eat light bulbs for assorted radio and TV programmes. If I didn't, they'd think I couldn't, so I complied, eating five light bulbs that day and being forced to eat lots of bananas until I shat a chandelier. It's true that it had been a Pepto-Bismol kind of day, but what had been barely more than indigestion turned into a fact-is-stranger-than-fiction blurb. The item ran on the front of the 'Scene' section of *USA Today*, major newspapers ran the bit, morning radio shows yucked it up. Jay Leno made fun of me that night; the next day I was fodder for Paul Harvey.

Talk of the circus was everywhere. The *Wall Street Journal* ran a cover story about us, including a drawing of me. Our video, taped in '92, had become a surprise hit, attracting a cult following. The kids were snatching it up at Tower

Records, and then memorizing the lines. People were throwing parties, turning the sound off and reciting the patter of the shows word for word. My campy presentation had struck a nerve. There was a national piercing craze, and some articles said we were behind it.

Now there were three sideshows in New York and two competing in Boston, and there was even one in Omaha, Nebraska, that called itself the Jim Rose Sideshow, and had a slug, a human pincushion and a lifto; in Portland there was a guy who billed himself a one-man Jim Rose show.

Posters advertising freaks I'd never met claimed TOURED WITH JIM ROSE SHOW, AND IS DESTINED FOR NATIONAL ACCLAIM! Those wacky morning radio shows started 'freak contests' as a self-promotional tool. Clubs advertised in glossy magazines: 'Friday and Saturday at midnight, dangerous sideshow stunts!' And many rock bands had made MTV videos that had carnival and sideshow themes.

On the one hand, I was elated: we'd helped to bring back a part of Americana to a Lost Generation whose only exposure to sideshows had been through books such as Katherine Dunn's *Geek Love* and *Freak Show* by Robert Bogdan. On the other hand, I was seeing history repeat itself. People think the sideshow died due to the advent of TV; but that's not entirely true. They vanished, I think, because so many popped up they were no longer unique. Now it was happening again. And we had added to the saturation by touring so much over the past two years. Were we just another one-hit wonder? Another Question Mark and the Mysterians with '96 Tears'? Everything pointed to the obvious: we needed a new show.

With all these new sideshows jumping in, how could we

outdo ourselves? Should I cut off an arm? I could only do that twice – and would need help the second time.

I didn't know what to do. Offers were winging my way to appear in shows and sitcoms. We'd been touring for two straight years, people were burned out, nerves were frayed and we hadn't made much money. We'd been struggling all this time for our art. I wasn't the only one contemplating early retirement. So we called a meeting.

I explained all the thoughts running around in my head, noting that when Barnum, years before, had been faced with similar questions, he had dumped sideshow and gone into

Roger Daltry, Eddie Vedder, Jim Rose.

circus. A successful troupe always stays a few steps ahead. We'd done a good job of presenting insanity's greatest hits, but now what? I felt the only way to be new again was to put together a show where skill combats danger: Thrills, Chills and Spills. An updated version of the daredevils you'd see in the late 60s at a World's Fair. 'Men,' I said, 'it's going to be a lot of hard work, and I can't guarantee success.'

By the end of the meeting Pincushion and Tube, the oldest members of the troupe, had decided to go back to their former jobs. My eyes turned to Enigma, Lifto and Bebe, who all said, 'Let's give it a go.'

Immediately I plunged into self-doubt. The old show had started out as fun – and evolved into professionalism. Due to expectations this one had to shine from the start. Especially since we had already booked an Australian tour, a mere eight weeks away, that now hung like a noose around my neck. What kind of stunts should we do? For inspiration I turned to the scrapbook filled with Bob Blackmar's photo collection. After looking at all that circus and sideshow history, I then took out my Rolodex and began flipping madly.

I flipped past the guy who blew the smoke out of his ear, the guy that poured dirt in his eyes, the Candle Lady, the Wikings.

By then word had leaked out that I was looking for new acts, and people started calling me – auditioning over the phone. One would-be circus member said he could chew tinfoil and annoy anyone with a cavity. Another suggested we pour Elmer's Glue-All over his body and let it dry. 'After it cracks,' he explained, 'I'll look like a human snake that's shedding.' I didn't want to burst his bubble by telling him I'd learned that from sideshows in the late 60s, when they pitched

it as the 'Alligator Man'. The calls kept coming: 'I can shove $6.25 up my nose, in quarters!!' boasted one interviewee. 'I can shove $8.50 up my nose in half-dollars!!' boasted another. I told them to keep their change, and kept scouting.

My fingers continued their trek through the freak pages, and I stopped on M, at 'Mark the Knife'. He was a knife thrower from Chicago who could also juggle chainsaws. I called him up and presented him with the offer of a stunt that had been mulling over in my head for some time. 'If you can balance a lawnmower on your chin,' I said, 'while people throw heads of cabbage at it, you're in.' He said he'd give it a try and get back to me.

Next stop: R – for 'Rubberman'. He'd told me back in San Francisco that he could pop his joints out and slither through the head of a tennis racquet, unstrung of course. (He didn't bill himself as Spaghetti Man.) We talked, and he said he'd consider it. God, I was depressed. People wouldn't even commit; they were only 'considering'.

While waiting for the circus to gel I was booked on *The Jon Stewart Show*. So I flew to his Manhattan studio, and while sitting around in the green room I got a call. It was Eddie Vedder, who was likewise in New York, and invited me to Carnegie Hall. Pearl Jam wasn't playing there; it was a celebration, Roger Daltry's fiftieth birthday, where Pete Townshend would play. Eddie must have known intuitively I was at one of my lowest points, and he sure knew how to boost my sagging spirits.

After taping the show with Jon I met Eddie in his private dressing room at Carnegie Hall. He'd brought a birthday cake, and on the way to deliver it to Roger I realized this was no ordinary night. Lou Reed and Sinéad O'Connor were

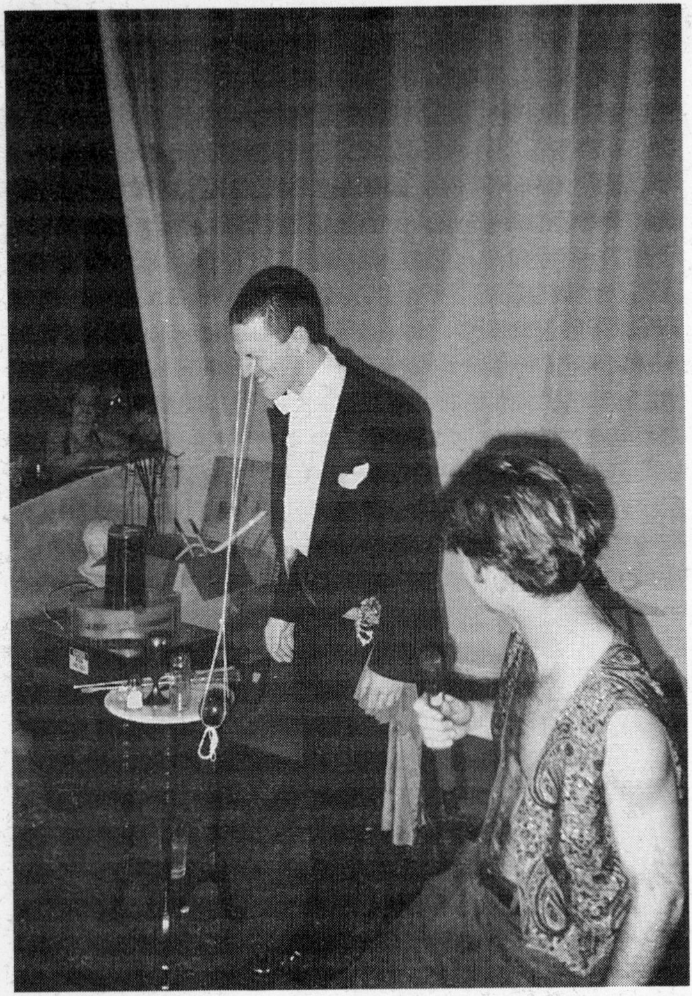

Slug and Jim Rose.
Photo by Lifto

there, as was my hero from freshman year in high school: Alice Cooper! I was like a little kid in his presence. Afterwards we went from bar to bar, and everywhere Eddie was mobbed. People would swarm him, holding up huge photos to be autographed – photos taken at the last bar that they'd had developed and enlarged at a one-hour photo stand. Fanaticism like that I'd never seen; he was barraged with propositions and adulation, and he periodically flashed glances of helplessness. I did my best at being a security guard, but quickly realized that you're only as famous as your last *Billboard* hit. Kids would have pushed aside Alice Cooper, Lou Reed, Roger Daltry and Pete Townshend just to get to Eddie. *A Hard Day's Night* finally made sense.

And so did our circus. Six days later, when I flew back, all the pieces fell in place: we had a new troupe. Mark the Knife agreed to join, and Rubberman called back with a double-jointed thumbs-up, allowing thrills and chills galore: Bebe the Circus Queen, who'd been practising for a few years, would walk up a ladder of razor-sharp swords barefoot, lie on a bed of nails in a bikini while people stood on her, and take electrocution to illuminate fluorescent lights held in her mouth. The Amazing Mr Lifto would continue his pierced weight-lifting, and added Super-Gluing a bowling ball to his hand, and enduring the explosion of hundreds of firecrackers taped to his bare chest. The Enigma slowly but surely was getting more blue, after establishing a network of the very best tattooists in the world, who donated their time to fill in a tattoo when we showed up in their town; at this point every other puzzle piece was blue. This work in progress was almost finished, a magnificent sight to behold. The Enigmatized One would swallow swords, eat glass, put a live scorpion in his

mouth, light a cigarette by sticking his face in a red-hot shower of sparks from an industrial grinder, lift heavy objects with hooks in his eye sockets and, as always, play keyboards. I would do face-in-glass, the razor-blade chomp, the straitjacket escape, a decompression challenge where I'd sit in a plastic bag with the air vacuumed out, eat dry ice to blow smoke rings from nose and mouth and, of course, be the simultaneous Human Blockhead and Dartboard.

We lined up the Zen Master Marky Ray, an awesome guitar player, who balanced a watermelon on his neck while I whacked it in half with a machete, and placed a sword to his toughened stomach and had audience members pound it in with a stick. He also lay on a bed of swords and had a concrete block busted on his chest with a sledgehammer, wielded by another new member – Bam Bam the Strongman, a purple-haired rocker of incredible strength who blew up a hot-water bottle until it exploded, stuck his hand in a raccoon trap and helped with the loading.

Mark the Knife, after risking a few dangerous haircuts, could now balance a running lawnmower on his chin while people pelted the rotating blades with cabbage. His other acts included juggling with two knives and a roaring chainsaw; he also threw knives around Bebe, the only troupe member fearless enough to try it. And the Rubberman was bringing his racquet.

We lined up a rehearsal studio at Moe, a recently opened club that featured the Rose Room – where our old banner hung over the bar, the Ali Baba sign took over a back wall and everywhere there were posters of tours we'd done from around the world.

Finally we'd meet in person these people who'd only

been voices on phones. We arranged a lunch, and surveyed the new troupe. They were a handsome bunch, young and energetic. The Rubberman mentioned how his parents had come from Armenia, so we gave him a new, more exotic name: the Armenian Rubberman. Then we headed to Moe for our first rehearsal. We rehearsed. And rehearsed. And rehearsed for two weeks. I was worried. We were awful. For two reasons: first, it felt like the old freak nights of yore; and secondly, we didn't have a must-see stunt, we needed that one big dick-kicker. I called a break, wrote, rewrote and rehearsed my presentations until I'd got it right. And since this show would feature power tools, I tried to conceive of a stunt that would incorporate machinery. Then it hit me: marry circus to sports – with chainsaw football. I envisioned the lights going out while performers ran around the audience with chainsaws blaring, making them scream like they would in a spookhouse, scaring the bejesus out of everyone in total darkness.

And just before the terror made them crap in their laps, the performers would run up to the stage, the lights would come on, they'd cut into wood to show the chainsaws were real, and then break out in a football scrimmage.

I knew in my gut that a darkened terrorist introduction to a chainsaw football game would be a hit; now I had to talk the Zen Master, Mark the Knife, Bam Bam and myself into doing it. They quickly agreed; I relented shortly thereafter. Once we grew accustomed to throwing and catching them, and had got over the fear of the noise, we put the chains back on and became the only players of the most dangerous sport in history. With the presentation in line, and a more exciting show than I'd envisioned two weeks before, we headed to Australia.

The first time I'd been there, with the old troupe, I was confident but was sick, and didn't enjoy it at all. This time I felt great, but was worried sick over how an audience would respond to the new show. It hadn't been time-tested.

The change in attitude towards us was immediate. We were actually being treated like a circus, not just freaks. Instead of calling us bug eaters, meat skewers and vomit drinkers, the press now hailed us as circus sports stars, snapping pictures of us with beloved rugby heroes. Every city we went to, the press had a field day when I challenged the local team to throw away that ball and use a chainsaw. 'Let's give a whole new meaning to 'halfback' and see who goes to the big locker room in the sky first!'

We stopped in at radio stations – where we chased the DJs with saws ablazing – and I barked, 'It's like a ten-ring circus! Things will be happening everywhere! High-flying, bone-jarring excitement! A ticket's good for a seat, but you'll use only the edge!'

Despite my on-air confidence I'd backed us into a pretty big corner. This show was new, I feared we were raw. And this was a rowdy country, where the locals toss dwarfs and box kangaroos. At least they were a fair lot, unlike the Wikings. The Aussies only took it out on you if you deserved it. I was afraid we would get what we deserved, when we pulled up to the theatre and saw a line coiling around the block.

An hour later the stage went dark. As soon as I heard the intro theme, the show immediately felt different. All the nights we'd burned the midnight oil had paid off. We started on a rock-'n'-roll note – with Zen Master in a kimono, wearing his hair in a Japanese-style ponytail, wailing on the guitar, with Enigma, clad in a fur suit that covered his head, leading

the way pounding keyboards.

We paraded through old acts at a mind-blowing speed. They went berserk for Lifto. They flipped over the new Enigma, who, once he'd ripped off his fur coat, scampered around the stage like an escaped beast. When Bebe the Circus Queen did the bed of nails – topless – they did backflips.

I knew that stuff would work. It was the new acts that concerned me. It was time for Zen Master to put down the guitar and do his stunts. 'Tonight,' I said into the mike, 'you will see two of the most severe martial-arts challenges. First he will expose himself to an oriental execution – *Shogun*-style – by placing a watermelon on the back of his neck and having it chopped in half with this machete. There will be no room for human error!'

I then picked up the gleaming machete 'Hiya-one, hiya-two, hwwooo-three.' *Whack!* the watermelon split in two. Zen Master got a bit of a shaver's escape, but nothing more. I made a note to try to stop the machete a hair's width sooner.

Bam Bam and Bebe brought out the bed of swords. 'And now,' I continued, 'Zen Master will lie on these, and have a concrete block placed on his chest, which will be beaten with a sledgehammer.' The Master reclined in a zen-like way on the swords, laid out like a wide-toothed silver comb, with the upturned edges pressing against his back. 'Three people in the last eleven years in South America did not survive,' I intoned eerily. 'Tonight, our entire circus holds their collective breath, knowing that career longevity is severely jeopardized by accepting this challenge.'

While Bam Bam placed the concrete block on Zenny's chest and picked up the sledgehammer, I snapped my fingers over the Zen Master's face. 'His eyes are shuttering, shuttering,

I no longer see pupil – only white. Eyes in the back of his head, trance-like.'

After lulling them into a beta state, I harshly screamed, 'BAM BAM THE STRONGMAN . . . Growing up in Seattle, chopping wood, he had no idea that he might be honing a skill to take a fellow-circus member's life.

'Quiet, here he goes.' *Crack*. Sledgehammer meets block. The audience sat there in dead silence. Until Zen Master's eyes fluttered, and he stood up. They did too – with wild applause. As he walked back to his guitar, I noticed he'd gotten a bit of a shaver's scrape, but nothing more. I made another note.

'As you know,' I said as the bed of swords was carried off, 'I've been all over the world, searching for the most bizarre humans I can find. Every year it changes. For 1994 this next man is it. Give it up for the Armenian Rubberman.'

The spotlight spilled on Rubberman, who waddled out on his knees, his body twisted like the caduceus climbing the Hippocratic staff. He stretched his arm out of the socket, and coiled it around his head like a turban. 'The Armenian Rubberman,' I whispered. 'He was not born like you or me. He's got a sock for a socket, and hair in places monkeys don't. He's a pretzel, A PRETZEL, a huuu-man bar snack. Watch him caress himself as only the Rubberman can. He switches arms so it feels like someone else. Why? Because he can.' Sometimes an old dog joke can come in handy.

'He's that crease in your wallet,' I pattered on. 'Look at the ribs on this huuu-man prophylactic. For safe sex you should always wear . . . a Rubberman. This man of elastic, standing six feet tall, will contract his frame – and slither through the head of this 1970s-model tennis racquet.'

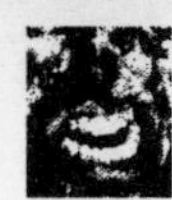

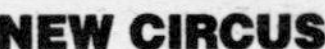

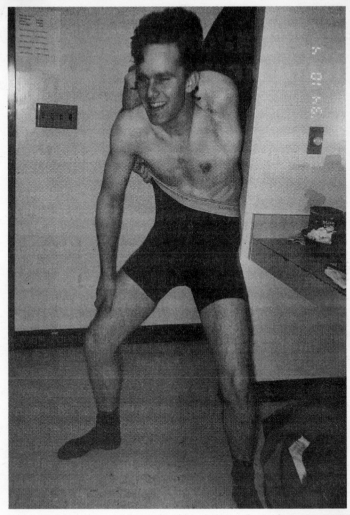

Rubberman.
Photo by Bebe Rose

At that point I draped the racquet over his head as through it were a medal. While the arm through the racquet stood straight up like the Statue of Liberty's, he hooked the other through the racquet. It caught at the shoulder; he popped it through. He was a quarter of the way there, as he writhed, and shoved his other shoulder in. Both arms extended above him, the racquet caught at the widest part of his upper torso, like a too-tight hula-hoop, as Rubberman began pulling on his chest skin and pushing the racquet down. 'If he gains a single pound,' I whispered, 'or becomes constipated, his career is over!'

He finally slammed the racquet over his chest, and it struck the hips. Discreetly, Rubberman turned his back to the audience, as he rearranged the part of him that's most rubber. 'The most difficult part of the anatomy,' I pointed out. 'How do you say "pop your balls" in Armenian, Rubberman?' He pushed the racquet down until it was half-assed. Grating the racquet past his prime, he meshed his manhood through and wriggled out. The screaming of girls pierced the air: 'Hey, what are you doing after the show?'

Mark the Knife ran onstage, clad in a screaming-orange monkey suit, clenching a handful of knives, with Bebe behind him, her lacy robe trailing. Bebe slipped off the robe and positioned herself, arms out, against a board the size of a mattress. The knife-throwing act always got to me. We all controlled our own stunts – except for this one. Bebe, my wife, the person I loved more than any other, was putting her entire body in his hands (so to speak), and nobody envied her for it. Nobody else volunteered for the job; every time she went on, I wished she'd never talked me into it.

The Knife began hurling his namesakes. *Slam!* A glistening blade landed inches from her right ear. *Slam!* A knife landed

millimetres from her neck. *Slam!* I couldn't look any more – every whack of the blade felt like it was hitting my heart.

As Bebe walked away, leaving her outline knifed in wood, Mark picked up a chainsaw, ran it through a log just to prove it was real, and balanced it on his chin. As he staggered and struggled with the roaring gasoline-powered shark that could make dog food of his face, it wavered, and seemed about to topple into the audience. Just when all the oxygen had been sucked out of the room with gasps, he caught it. He threw it up in the air, grabbed two machetes and started to juggle. While the crowd cheered and heaved sighs of relief, I said, 'For this next stunt, no one can stand up. Things will be flying over your heads. If someone comes too close to you, scream so they can hear you and will know to back away. And now I want to introduce you to the Jim Rose Chainsaw Stunt Team!'

The lights went out. It was completely dark. Meanwhile Bam Bam and Lifto had gone around, snuck into the back of the audience, let their chainsaws rip and raced through the aisles. It's one of those late-twentieth-century phobias: there's nothing like a power tool coming your way in the dark to put the fear of God into you. You could feel the wind when all heads in the audience snapped backwards, and they braced themselves against chairs. Just as the audience were clasping their hands to pray, all hell broke loose. Enigma bolted towards them, waving a siren with a red flasher. Bebe and Rubberman grabbed high-powered squirt guns and spritzed the audience with cold water. Mark the Knife continued terrorizing the front rows with his chainsaw, and he was even scarier in the dark. All the while I'd yell into the mike, 'Scream if they get too close.' Screams begat screams.

The lights came on, and we put away all but one chainsaw, to be used in a lively and deathly game of football. We huddled, hiked and passed until a touchdown was scored. To celebrate the points, Mark the Knife picked up a roaring lawnmower, balanced it on his chin, and we tossed heads of cabbage at it – leaving the entire stage covered in cabbage.

We took a bow, and when I looked up the entire audience was standing and cheering. One of the happiest sights of my life. As I walked off the stage, this show felt like the perfect blend of classic stunts combined with the new, and I chanted in my head silently, We did it, we did it!

I had scheduled the tour to break in the new circus, and had made sure we had plenty of time between shows to relax and take in the sights. Being such a huge chunk of land, Australia had it all: beaches, mountains, deserts, kangaroos and Aboriginals. I met one on the Gold Coast. He threw a metal boomerang the length of two soccer fields; when it whipped back he caught it – with his teeth! Now I knew why airline security in Australia considered a boomerang a deadly weapon.

The Down Under tour was over the top. Sold-out shows, appearances on prime-time TV, press everywhere. Networks even made us offers for our own show. We loved that country; someday Bebe and I may take them up on it. But at that point Australian television would have to wait. Because Scotland was next on our agenda. The Edinburgh Festival, again.

After weeks of stressing over new stunts we finally had a full wind in our sails, and a feeling of vindication. But we had an old wall to hurdle: the British press – those fickle members of the media who love to build people up just to smash them down. How would they treat us this year? Would they like us bloodless, bileless and bugless?

Our answer came immediately, but we didn't know it. It was staring us right in the face the day we came to town. Newspaper vendors pick their favourite headline of the day and post it on sandwich boards. And everywhere we went the sidewalk signs advertising newspapers screamed FLYMO FURIOUS!! (We had no idea that they were talking about us. Flymo is the Kleenex of tissue, the Vaseline of petroleum jelly, in the UK lawnmower world.)

The press had got wind of our new chin-balanced cabbage shredder – and had contacted the Flymo lawnmower company asking if ours was a safe usage. To judge by their comments Flymo was as ticked as Super Glue had been the year before.

In town and ready to play the game, we called a press conference. When asked, I said, 'Take your Flymo out of that cobwebbed shed, and wheel it into the kitchen! Flymo should sponsor us! We're showing consumers a whole new use!' (Sound familiar?)

Flymo preferred that we did not use their name in the show, so I said, 'I can't believe Flymo doesn't want us to use the name of their Flymo lawnmower when the Flymo is balanced on a chin and becomes a Flymo dice-a-matic. Flymo!'

Predictably, our friend the Conservative council woman butted her way into the press and once again called for a banning. In Great Britain's quirky way it's all in good fun, and sells massive amounts of tickets. Eleven thousand paid $15 to see us, almost doubling the number from the year before. I've never met a more helpful politician in my life.

While in Edinburgh we received an unexpected call from my agent back home, Branigan. 'Nine Inch Nails wants you to open for them,' Branigan crowed into the phone. I'd been hearing lots about the band – pictures of the disturbingly

handsome headman Trent Reznor were slapped across the pages of all the rock magazines, which were packed with praise about his latest release, 'The Downward Spiral'. The music was industrial – weird noises with a beat that's in the same genre as Ministry; but instead of looking like a biker, Trent looked like a masochistic ghost. Their words were dark, their music haunting and Trent was portrayed as moody.

Nine Inch Nails wanted us to tour the US with them. At first I was psyched, then troubled. We really liked their music, and of course we liked the idea of playing for the biggest crowds of our career. But Nine Inch Nails . . . they had a reputation for wreaking havoc on all they touched. For example, us.

We were supposed to have brushed up against them six months earlier in Tucson, as an opening act. When we got to Arizona, they were nowhere to be found. The night before, Trent had thrown a mike stand into the air and it landed on the drummer's face, knocking him unconscious and leaving a gash that required stitches. They'd cancelled the show we were supposed to play at. I'm used to people who are insane for a living, but not someone who's just insane. They seemed so unpredictable. If we booked a tour with them, and it was cancelled, our circus could go bankrupt.

Branigan assured me they rarely cancelled, and they loved to tour. And he said this was going to be one of the biggest productions of the year. 'You won't believe how their set is decorated,' he said, 'and the light show's rockin'. Trent took all the money he made from the soundtrack of *Natural Born Killers* and gave it back to his fans. This thing is an event!'

With great reservation I agreed to signing up with the Nine Inch Nails tour – knowing that they could make our circus extinct. We braced ourself for an ice age.

NINE INCH NAILED

uncie, Indiana. September 1994. I was sitting on a packing crate backstage at Ball State University, writing a set list amid broken-down, folded-up basketball hoops. From the shadows of nets a dark figure approached.

It was Trent Reznor. The master of Nine Inch Nails, the man who had bought the house where Sharon Tate was killed. The guy who'd invited us on this tour. The prince of destruction.

I looked up, expecting to see someone in need of an exorcist. Instead I saw a guy with a shy smile and honest eyes, delicate features and inky black hair, who seemed so composed, so elegant, and so striking that he might have stepped out of a Renaissance painting.

'Hey, Jim,' he said, extending his pale hand. 'Happy you're here.' He was neither cocky nor demented, but soft-spoken and completely relaxed.

I, on the other hand, was freaking. Here we were an hour away from opening for NIN, perhaps the most outrageous

Nine Inch Nails, US Tour 1994.
Photo by Bebe Rose

band of the late twentieth century. Trent was the main buzz of music magazines – and the celebrity ones too, all of which painted a picture of him as moody, brooding, sullen, tortured and slightly maniacal. Qualities I happen to like, and so apparently did the listening public, but that might have had more to do with his mesmerizing music. His following was huge: I've lived in towns with fewer residents than the people out there in Ball State's arena.

My mouth flew open, and I heard my voice croak out, sounding even more hyper than usual. 'You know, Trent,' I said, gnawing on my thumbnail, 'I'm scared to death. At Lollapalooza we played the second stage. These crowds are

going to be our biggest audiences ever. I mean, Trent, before this we were just *Sanford and Son.* Now we feel like *The Jeffersons.*'

Just as I was saying '-sons', an amoeba-like crowd surrounded Trent, engulfed him and swept him away. That brief encounter was the closest I'd get to him for days.

We headed to our dressing room, which was brimming with catering trays, wine, cocktails and exotic beers. First-class all the way. This place even had a shower. And towels.

Suddenly there was a huge racket coming from next door, and we ran over to investigate. It was Marilyn Manson – in the midst of a pre-show trashing of their dressing room as they filed out to the stage.

They were a fetching sight. First off, Marilyn Manson is a man – as beautiful as Monroe, as sinister as Charlie. Tall, lanky, with long dark hair, he wore a different-coloured tigeresque contact in each eye, and lipstick was smeared from the bottom of his nose to half-way down his chin. His every tooth was blackened, intentionally; this wasn't just one tooth blacked out like on *Hee Haw.* Paling his face was the whitest make-up you could find this side of a chalk factory. There was something instantly charismatic about this walking cadaver.

He was the front man, ushering the shock rock tradition of Alice Cooper, Kiss and Iggy Pop into the 90s. And when he took to the stage, Marilyn's Manson streak came out: he bared his teeth like a Rottweiler and broke into 'Cake and Sodomy' – taking breaks between lyrics to spit on the audience. His moves and gyrations entranced the cowering crowd, who stared wide-eyed as if they'd just found their leader, between ducks and grimaces.

After listening to one song we had to leave to check and

recheck all our props. It's that nervous ritual that opens every tour, but it was executed all the more nervously tonight.

Despite the hundreds of shows we'd done by then, we were antsy. There were seventeen thousand people out there. And every single one of them wanted to see Nine Inch Nails. Knowing our name was the Jim Rose Circus, we'd decided to do a faster, meaner and rawer show to bridge the gap between us and the Nails as quickly as possible.

We darted on to the stage and zipped through at a mind-numbing speed. Out of the corner of my eye I could see Trent watching us from the wings – and that made me talk even faster. A forty-five-minute set felt like we'd jogged on, lapped around the stage and run off. It must have been slightly more entertaining than that, because the crowd proved their appreciation by giving us all the *oohhs* and *aahhs* at the right times.

As we walked off, applause singing in our ears, we were ecstatic. Electricity zapped through the air. I'd thought it was because we'd done well, but soon realized the real reason: everyone backstage was looking at Trent, walking down the hall. Wherever he walked, people seemed to ionize and knock into another orbit.

Our set over, we now lurked in the wings – to watch this man with the supposedly bad attitude, who had been so nice, to see what all the hoopla was about. At the time I was feeling pretty jaded about music. Rock 'n' roll was actually starting to bore me, and I was considering a change to country-western. This show, I figured, would be the one to put me over the edge, and I mentally reviewed how to do do-si-dos.

The curtains onstage were closed, and bathed in a white light, when eerie Gothic music pierced the air with a drumbeat

that sounded like the rhythmic clanging inside a steel mill. It went on for minutes – building the drama. Then the smoke machine transformed the entire stage into one big puff; green lights hit the clouds, creating a lime fog. It felt like a street corner in a Batman movie. The music went hyper as the curtains began to part. The second it opened, Trent ran right for the mike, leaving the band to be gradually unveiled with each pulling of the curtain rope.

With total abandon he transformed himself right before my eyes into a cat in need of a spay, a ravenous dog, a wanton beast of some kind ripping his heart out, his guts, his soul, and then stomping on them. He fell to his knees and wrapped his arms around the mike, as if reunited with an old flame.

This man was a spectacle, a runaway train, and he was turning the crowd into a herd of stampeding bulls, knocking each other over. Trent was their leader in the china shop, kicking keyboards and toppling drum sets, while an army of stagehands followed in his wake, trying to reassemble what this amplified tornado had undone. It was a tantrum one could only dream of having. He seemed to have the attitude that he could do whatever he wanted, whenever he wanted – and did.

His act was the epitome of dysfunctional: he pounded us with the hardest melodies, he lulled us into the depths of melancholy, and then pummelled us all over again. And he was doing everything so fast. His show was a ship in a storm, as unpredictable as nature or a woman with really bad PMS.

When he was sad, he was crying; when he was hard, he kicked mike stands and instruments, breaking them into pieces. During the second song he grabbed the guitar player, picked

him up, carried him to the edge of the stage and tossed him – instrument and all – into the moshing masses.

It felt like a war-torn battle zone; I took a step back. And decided to postpone the country-western phase.

This guy wasn't just a media hypester lacking substance or form. He was for real: bringing together looks, brilliant music, incredible lyrics, a stage energy that shook all who watched, and winding up everyone with a musical lasso that never slacked or relaxed. Even when he was just standing at the mike, you knew his toes were kneading the stage. Trent had more talent and charisma in his earlobe than any whole human I'd ever seen.

At this point, weighing the image of the person I'd met backstage with the fury onstage, I realized Trent was a human dichotomy: you never knew what he would do next, but whatever it was, it would be honest and from the gut. With the integrity he displayed onstage he immediately made me trust him, and made it plain to me why everyone stared when he walked by. Branigan was right: this tour was an event.

I was truly in awe and realized he possessed a combination of qualities that few humans are aware they have: true talent with hot-blooded conviction. This was a man with a vision on a mission. He made a believer out of me. I made a note to do the next night's show twice as fast.

After the set, as did everyone else there, I felt like a sieve, all energy drained through me. It struck me as impossible that Trent could even do the show the next night.

Then it hit me like a flying mike stand: the reason he's so relaxed and soft-spoken pre-performance is he's saving up every ounce of his energy so he can explode in his two-hour show.

Knives thrown around Jim Rose.
Photo by Danny Clinch, 1994

When the band got off, they were whisked away to shower up before that night's festivities started. After the band had scrubbed behind their ears, the OK was given to let the party roll. I was elated at the thought that we were going to hang with Trent, and we could talk about performance, passion and drive – and I could tell him exactly how much he moved me, a topic that had never seemed necessary before.

All the people with the VIP passes – namely Marilyn Manson and the circus – paraded into the Nine Inch Nails

dressing room. Their dressing room was catered three times higher and wider than our dressing room, and the selection of beers was three times as exotic, though everybody seemed to be drinking Bud and Rolling Rock. When we slunk in, the band was still in the shower room putting on their clothes; this being a nightly routine of merriment, they weren't rushing. As soon as Trent walked out and into the party, that amoeba crowd engulfed him again and he was swarmed. As soon as two walked out of the pack surrounding him, three others replaced them.

Getting to Trent would take a two-by-four, or at least a chainsaw. The man whom we were touring with, who so inspired me each time he took the stage, was a stranger.

For weeks our only contact was exchanging pleasantries as we walked offstage and he walked on. I didn't want more than that; it seemed like there were always dozens of people chewing on his ear. He was approachable, but he seemed so burdened, we just left him alone.

Then one night Trent and a friend strode out of the NIN dressing room, a stun gun in hand. 'Hey, Jim,' Trent said, 'Jerry here says he can take the shock. Can anybody in your circus do that?' Overhearing this, modest Mr Lifto yelled, 'Hell, you can stun-gun my dick.'

It was the *Titanic* moment, the one that broke the ice. That night Trent and I sat off in one of the side rooms and swapped war stories about life on the road. I told him about the French Fiasco, the Montreal Bloodfest, the Wikings. He told me about his days as a janitor at a recording studio in Cleveland, trading his hours pushing a broom for time to record his music.

It was a drunken, bonding moment, especially when I told him about having had crossed eyes, and he swore he couldn't see my bald spot.

He told me that he too had once been a freak: as a kid he was plagued with auditory problems and was forced to wear tubes sticking out of his ears. For years he was tormented and treated as an alien.

Hours and many tales later I left Trent as I always do: happy and confused. Over the following weeks I found that the only thing I liked more than telling a good story was listening to one of his. He always knew how to make me laugh. And he actually knew how to make me shut up.

We were on the road for five months, and night after night it was one big party, interrupted for those forty-five minutes when we had to perform; there were only four more interruptions to go until we had a two-week Christmas break. Two of those interruptions were at Madison Square Garden, which bills itself correctly as the most famous arena in the world. Both NIN shows sold out within an hour.

The first show was cancelled, when the band's bus crashed and the guitarist sprained his finger. The second show was a mobhouse, press, celebs, limos everywhere. Larry 'Bud' Melman put in an appearance, even shuffling out on the stage to say, 'Boy, that Jim Rose Circus sure gives me a watery pig's eye. And now for the other side of the anatomy, Nine Inch Nails will punch your balls off.' Larry certainly knew how to read off cue cards.

After their close brush with death the night before, the Nails set was particularly destructive that night, turning the stage into splinters and shards of metal.

As we walked offstage towards the bus for our final show, I felt that electricity zapping the air again and looked up to see JFK Junior – waiting to meet Trent.

This leg of the tour was capped off in Philadelphia,

where we all said Merry Christmas until four in the morning. A camaraderie had built up between us, and I almost felt teary-eyed realizing I'd be separated for over a week from the guys who by now felt like kin.

The next day I arrived in Seattle – just long enough to sidle up next to that *Newsweek* stringer Melissa Rossi, whom I'd brought in to help write this book, before I knew the circus would spend the whole year on the road. She was looking that frayed, greenish way she always does under deadline, but assured me that in the few days remaining before due date we could finish the task before us.

We spent the holidays gathered around her computer, drinking eggnog, eating pears and every so often breaking into song just to keep our spirits high, since we were missing every holiday bash in the city. For Christmas we took a quick break to eat borscht, then headed back to the computer again. In no time the job was nearly complete.

No sooner had the troupe headed back on the road than the tour somehow became wilder than ever. Playing in Long Island, Trent brought out one of my heroes, Adam Ant, to play the encore – and Adam dedicated it to the circus. Minutes later Howard Stern loped into our dressing room to shake hands – though in fact, given the height difference between us, it would have been easier for me to shake his knee. Even though he was talking down to me, it never felt like he was, and I've never taken a quicker liking to a media personality. The next day the king of shock radio was talking about us over the air, saying stuff so sweet even the Enigma was blushing, making his blue skin turn sort of purple.

And then it was that blur syndrome that happens after a year on the road: all life is reduced to a blur of arenas, parties,

motels and Denny's, where I'd call in at 3 a.m. for an editing session. Through it all Trent remained the calm and collected destructo king – the kind of guy who could probably move mountains with a mean glance. One night the troupe was sitting backstage with the roadies and some of the crew. NIN wasn't around, and it wasn't the night for *Murder, She Wrote*, so we were all pretty bored, as we downed more beer and chomped on sandwiches, gazing at the door that had one of those green exit signs hanging over it.

Suddenly, out of nowhere, an apple slammed the green exit sign. It was the end of a six-month tour; such innocent rowdiness was to be expected. Besides, the sign didn't break. A minute later the apple was followed by an orange, and a beer can. Still it didn't break. This was a challenge; for the next five minutes everyone pelted it, with sandwiches, plates, bottles – the air was filled with flying debris. And still the light wouldn't break. Finally, someone threw a metal casserole dish and the plastic cover of the light broke off. However, the bulk of the sign remained firmly entrenched in its spot. The mission then became to knock it out of the ceiling. Someone threw one of those standing metal ashtrays. Didn't faze it. People started throwing chairs, tables, mike stands, even the couch that we'd been sitting on until then. It was still hanging, sort of crooked, but hanging. The damn thing wouldn't fall. We'd run out of stuff to throw at it.

About then Trent strode in, holding a coffee cup, to see what all the noise was about. He looked up at the exit sign, by then hanging by a string, and surveyed the crap under it that by now was piled just about as high as the sign. With a shrug he nonchalantly tossed the coffee cup at the exit sign. It came crashing down. The prince of destruction still reigns.

The Jim Rose Circus Sideshow 1995.
Photo by Mark Nouillan

And somehow the little circus that thought it could (for at least a month or two) is still chugging. It's a strange way to make a living, and my dentist has made me cut down on eating light bulbs, but I'm never bored and have never had more fun in my life.

Which brings us to the present, at the edge of the future, which I'm sure will be full of jolts. Because you do not get old when you stop skipping down the sidewalk flailing your arms. You start to age when you don the green eyeshades and think you've seen it all. The fountain of youth is found simply in believing that something amazing could be whipping around the next corner. Just watch out – it might be a high-speed crashing exit sign.

And now that most of my dreams have been realized, for this month at least, if I could just get some sleep.

JIM ROSE QUESTION & ANSWER

What's the one trick you wish you could do?

A running lawnmower balanced on my chin with audience members throwing heads of lettuce at it while I'm juggling chainsaws, all at the same time.

What does Mr Lifto's willy look like?

A baby's arm holding an apple.

Describe the Torture King in three words.

Smart, quiet, enduring.

What wouldn't you allow in your circus?

Predictability.

What was your worst accident?

Three people fell on top of me while I was lying on a bed of nails.

How often do you rehearse?

Never. Who would want to rehearse the human dartboard?

When was the last time someone threw up in front of you?

Every night.

What do you consider dangerous?

Censorship.

DON'T TRY THIS AT HOME!

SWORD-SWALLOWING

This is a fine example of how bodies can be altered, and how you can trick the natural order. Sword swallowers tickle their gag reflexes seven times a day for three years until they stop gagging. Once the reflex no longer responds, they can shove a sword down the oesophagus into the stomach effortlessly.

To tickle the reflex they typically start by sticking a finger down their throat, until they just about throw up. They do it again, again and again, until they can slide their finger down with no response. After that, they use a dull fencing sword, pushing it down as far as they can, gradually getting it down farther and farther. After years the body is modified, and once it stops responding to foreign intruders such as swords, the skill is achieved.

FIRE-EATING

Half of this act is making the torches. Fire eaters take cotton strings off a mop, tighten them into a ball with copper wire, and affix the ball around the end of a coat hanger. The ball is then dipped into lighter fuel.

Once the torch is lit, fire eaters lick their lips, make sure their mouth is moist and arch their head back as far as it can go, so that the flames they're sticking towards their mouth are going upward. They never breathe in during this or they'd be breathing fire down their throat. The key is to breathe out slowly – slowly enough so as not to put the flames out. They continue breathing slowly out of their mouth as the fire is lowered past their lips and into their oral cavity. They give one last puff of air and close their lips - *extinguishing it in the process.*

REGURGITATION

Thousands of people have wondered how Houdini used to break out of jails. One of his secrets was that he could swallow a key to the top of the gag reflex, and bring it back up at will. I do this with razor blades.

This skill relies on modifying the swallowing process. Regurgitators use an experience common to everyone. If you have taken too big a bite, and it gets stuck in your throat, you have to work it up slowly but surely. Regurgitators tease and provoke this mechanism, practising first with objects that are not harmful – such as big pieces of bread.

PIERCED WEIGHT-LIFTING

With the glut of piercers, anyone who wants his or her body parts pierced must be careful. This stunt demands a piercer who is very experienced, because infections are a pierced weight lifter's worst enemy. Those who pierce their tongue discover that it thickens, making eating or talking difficult for weeks. Ears are pretty normal; nipples are fine. For piercing the penis, the best way to go is under the head – so the ring goes there and out where you pee.

Once they have these piercings, practitioners must keep an object inserted so the holes don't close. They add large-gauged jewellery to widen the holes, in the same way that Africans do. The holes are gradually stretched larger and larger. Once the holes have got to a size that can take hooks, they attach the hooks to a light chain and to objects they want to lift. The weight lifter's goal is to callous the areas that take the weight. So they start with something small, then get heavier and heavier – and more impressive. They add heavier-gauge chain along the way, which helps to make the stunt look more impressive. As all pierced weight lifters can tell you, they put up with large amounts of discomfort for many years to perfect their art.

STRAITJACKET ESCAPE

Unfortunately, there are fake devices that can give their users' audience the illusion of witnessing a human marvel. Some people buy fake swords that collapse when they're pushed in – a trick whose widespread use dims the lustre of the true masters. The same holds for straitjackets: there are gimmick ones available that anybody can get out of. Real straitjackets, however, are still available and can be ordered through the Humane Restraint Company out of Waunakee, Wisconsin. Contrary to popular belief an escape artist doesn't pop a shoulder to get out. This stunt relies on a pretzel movement of the arm: escape artists put one arm over the head, and the other one behind their back, and curlicue out of it. An insane person wouldn't figure that out; but straitjacket escape is relatively easy for those who can understand the pretzel logic.

WALKING ON HOT COALS

Certain self-help groups have been using this feat as the ultimate self-confidence booster. The fact is this is one of the easiest of all the Hindu, yogi and fakir feats. It's a simple procedure – the coals are allowed to get red, red, red hot, then semi-white. They are measured out, so it takes five steps or less to get across the coals. Coal walkers move rapidly over the white coals, since their feet must be off within seven seconds before the heat registers. A cheater alternative: some use volcanic rock, which doesn't retain the heat that coals do and actually look more impressive to the unitiated.

THE HUMAN BLOCKHEAD

A human blockhead is someone who pounds something – usually a spike or a nail – into his face. He takes advantage of the public's general lack of anatomical knowledge. In each nostril there are two nasal cavities – one that goes up and one that goes straight back into the head. Blockheads use the second one. They have to get over the impulse to sneeze; that's where the danger comes in.

A blockhead often starts with a small nail and roots around in his nose, familiarizing himself with the terrain and the two different passages. Once he finds the one that goes straight into his face, he begins sticking small nails up there, and ultimately wide nails or screwdrivers. From there it's a matter of getting over the watery eyes and the desire to sneeze.

EATING A GLASS LIGHT BULB

First of all, glass eaters never bite into a light bulb with their teeth; the bulb is always broken by someone else, such as an audience member.

Light bulb glass is usually very thin, although we've been in some countries where it's quite thick, which caused a bit of a problem, and indigestion. What glass eaters do is to chew softly – so they are breaking the glass up, and it's not popping on to their gums and tongue, creating cuts.

After chewing the shards softly down to small fragments, the glass eater shifts the glass to his molars and chews with more authority. The goal is to try to chew the glass back into sand – which is what glass is made from. Once the shards are particle-sized, he swallows, with little danger to his stomach. The stomach can feel a little sandpapery the next morning.

However, this stunt can pose a problem for glass eaters with cavities or sensitive teeth (and eating glass strips enamel off teeth). Great as an occasional party trick, this act is too hard on the teeth to be a nightly stunt.

THE HUMAN PINCUSHION

The maxim here is 'If you can pinch an inch of skin, you can stick through a pin.' Professional pincushions typically ram needles and skewers through their arms, legs, throats, chests, cheeks and eyebrows – anywhere they can lift extra skin. Their key: don't ram the needles through the vein and capillary system; and, when pulling needles out, pull slowly, giving any blood that may have formed time to coagulate.

Pincushions typically start with pins, then hatpins, then skewers – gradually using thicker piercers as their body becomes accustomed to the jabs. Most cushions gradually develop, much like a worn tennis racquet, a sweet spot on their body, and can eliminate the original discomfort associated with this act.

THE YOGA RIBBON STUNT

During this act someone, typically a yogi, will eat a ribbon, go through stomach gyrations, then pull out the ribbon from the hole in his abdomen, making it appear as though it's gone the fast track through the digestive system. However, this stunt is generally based on an illusion. Typically the performer already has a tunnelled hole into his abdomen, situated an inch to the left of the belly button. And in that hole he has placed a second identical ribbon, which he pulls out after swallowing the first ribbon.

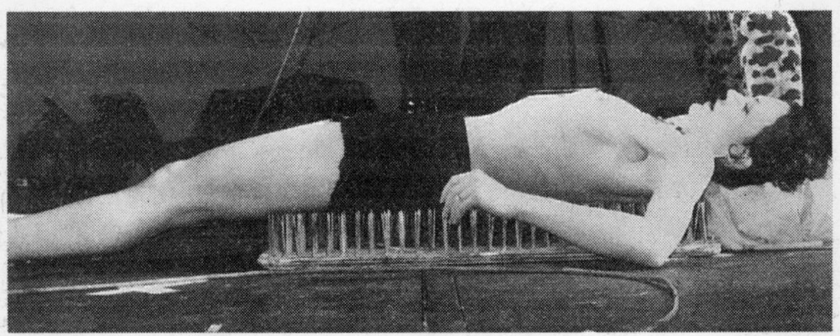

Bebe the Circus Queen on a bed of nails.